HUMAN RESOURCE MANAGEMENT ISSUES IN
DEVELOPING COUNTRIES

Human Resource Management Issues in Developing Countries

Edited by
FARHAD ANALOUI
Development and Project Planning Centre
University of Bradford

Routledge
Taylor & Francis Group

LONDON AND NEW YORK

First published 1998 by Ashgate Publishing

Reissued 2018 by Routledge
2 Park Square, Milton Park, Abingdon, Oxon, OX14 4RN
711 Third Avenue, New York, NY 10017, USA

Routledge is an imprint of the Taylor & Francis Group, an informa business

Publisher's Note
The publisher has gone to great lengths to ensure the quality of this reprint but points out that some imperfections in the original copies may be apparent.

Disclaimer
The publisher has made every effort to trace copyright holders and welcomes correspondence from those they have been unable to contact.

A Library of Congress record exists under LC control number: 98072802

ISBN 13: 978-1-138-32027-7 (hbk)
ISBN 13: 978-0-429-45341-0 (ebk)

Contents

List of tables and figures

List of contributors

Pauline M. Amos-Wilson Principle Lecturer, Oxford Brooks University. She is currently the Manager for the MBA Programme.

Dr. A. R. Analouei is currently with InfoPro as a Group Manager and has previously held key managerial positions including, Associate Professor of Research, Georgetown University, U.S.A.

Dr. Farhad Analoui Senior Lecturer, Director of Professional Development and Training Programmes, Development Project Planning Centre, University of Bradford, UK.

John Cusworth Senior Lecturer, Head of the Department, Development and Project Planning Centre, University of Bradford.

Derek Eldridge Lecturer, Institute for Development and Policy Management, University of Manchester.

Dr. Hossein Jalilian Lecturer, Development and Project Planning Centre, University of Bradford, UK.

Ernita Joaquin Researcher in the Local Government Centre, College of Public Administration, University of the Philippines.

S. Tene Kaminski Lecturer, Bolton Business School, Bolton, UK.

Oriel Kenny Lecturer, Development and Project Planning Centre, University of Bradford, UK.

John Launder Lecturer, Development and Project Planning Centre, University of Bradford.

Dr. Pete Mann Lecturer, Institute for Development and Policy Management, University of Manchester.

Dr. Farhad Noorbakhsh Senior Lecturer, Centre for Development Studies, University of Glasgow, UK.

Y. Yashar Sentürk Doctoral Research Student, Development and Project Planning Centre, University of Bradford. Research Officer, University of Aberdeen, UK.

Harry Wes Research Associate, Graduate Business School, University of Strathclyde. He is a Fellow of the Institute of Personnel and Development.

Preface

People are no longer viewed as mere input to closed system organisations, occupying well defined isolated roles, and working and living in a relatively stable environment. The mechanistic notions of managing people in a controlled context have rapidly become a thing of the past. Today in a changing environment in which socio-economic factors are but only one major changing factor, the accepted reality is also that of changing expectations of people from organisations, in addition to the presence of fierce competition in an unstable market economy towards meeting the demands of an uncertain future. In such precarious circumstances human resources constitute the most important factor, should the organisation be interested in their long term, continued survival and development.

The complexity of organisational interface with one another, and the explosion of information technology, in addition to changing expectations in the workplace, makes Personnel Management (PM) with its limited role, an increasingly redundant concept. The midddle ground position of PM between the management and the employees not only implies that they assume a devisive role which draws a distinction between management and the employee, it also places disproportionate emphasis on exercising external control and meeting the short term needs of their organisation and its resources. Human Resource Management (HRM), on the other hand, sees the organisation from a holistic perspective, an integrated system within an interrelated network of local, national and international organisations.

One of the major aspects of HRM, not surprisingly, is the Development of Human Resources with the strategic view of meeting future needs and demands of the organisation. Thus, assuming a far greater role than paying attention not only to maintaining the status quo by employing and training employees and being responsible for their welfare, rather than being engaged in the proactive process of forecasting, planning and developing strategies to develop the human resources needed to meet the future demands. The issues of quality therefore are no longer discussed only in relation to the product and services of an enterprise, but in the context of learning organisations with change cultures and work life relationships.

The vast field of HRM and its related issues however, has posed a challenge for the academics and scholars who assume the role of providers of know-how for the practitioners in the development field. At the Development and Project Planning Centre (DPPC), University of Bradford, this need and necessity has long been realised. The formation of a research cluster in Human Resource Management and Development in 1993 was a response to this need. The international seminar held in March 1996 and subsequent International Conference which was held at the Centre in 1997 allowed greater participation and involvement of both scholars and practitioners to explore HRM issues and share their understandings and experiences of human development.

Farhad Analoui
Senior Lecturer

Acknowledgements

I wish to acknowledge the contribution made by so many individuals who have been either directly or indirectly involved in the preparation of the present volume. In particular, I would like to thank Pauline Fell who organised the conference which provided the basis for the present collection of papers. Also, thanks are due to Jean Hill for the production of many drafts of the manuscript, Sue Mackrill for assisting with the print of the final camera - ready copy of the work and finally, my wife Janet Analoui for the reading through the text and her constructive and detailed comments and suggestions.

I am grateful to the authors for their contributions to this volume and for accepting to make their work available to other students, scholars and practitioners so that a better understanding of the subject can be gained. Of, course the reader ought to bear in mind that what is presented in each chapter, forms the views of the authors and the authors alone and does not in any way represent the views of a particular organisation, institute or agency with which they are associated.

Finally, I would like to thank Professor Brenda Costall, Pro Vice Chancellor for her support and encouragement and to acknowledge the efforts of the members of the Human Resource Management Development Research Cluster at the DPPC, University of Bradford for their support and contribution.

1 Managerial perspectives, assumptions and development of the human resource management

Farhad Analoui

Introduction

What follows in this chapter enables the reader, student, managers (practitioners) and academics alike, to gain a basic but fundamental understanding of how the dominant views and concepts in management (Perspectives) have been developed. What are the main assumptions about for example, 'task' and 'people' and what is their relevance for the emergence of concepts such as 'Personnel Management' (PM) and Human Resource Management' as an umbrella for development of the human resources in context of the work organisations?

To achieve this, the major milestones in the development of the perspectives in management will be examined. Also an exploration of the theories X, Y and Z, which have been the main assumptions behind the development of managerial thoughts will be included. And how these theories formed the basis for the development of a need for PM or HRM, of which HRD forms a significant part, will be discussed in some detail. Finally, relevant conclusions will be reached.

The development of management

While it is unnecessary to follow every detail of the evolutionary process of how management as it is today was created and established, it is essential to become familiar with the milestones in the process: each of which reveals the philosophy, value structure, beliefs and most importantly the dominant

1

assumptions which were held by scholars, theorists, developers, trainers and practitioners at different points in time.

Each milestone in the development of management is marked by a new or rather a different set of assumptions about the nature of the work, organisations, people, clients and other concepts such as motivation, reward and the like. Although, at first glance, to the students and practitioner, there seems to be almost no unifying structure for relating the various ideas, concepts and skills in management, the underlying presuppositions and practices provide the basis for rather distinctive perspectives on management. The stress ought to be placed on the overlapping nature of schools of thoughts and perspectives from which the world of work, people and organisations have been looked at and on the fact that each perspective in management provides a basis for the development of the next and the changing ways which have been used to deal with people as resources in organisations.

Perspectives in management

In order to understand the perspectives from which the concept of management has been viewed, created and even promoted, it is necessary to see the inseparable link between management as a discipline and the parallel developments in other disciplines such as organisational studies and sociology, industrial psychology, economics, personnel and human resource management, accountancy and the world of finance. The closest related subject to management is that of organisation and organisational studies (Silverman, 1970; Burrell and Morgan, 1979). The term organisations nowadays, can be employed to describe the personal attention which is given to matters related to the individuals own life and general development, however, when it comes to 'management' it would be unjust to claim that the presence of one (organisation) necessitates the existence of the other (London, 1978).

Organisations, unlike business, administration and projects in the established or temporary states, arise when individuals and groups each pursue their own interests, but also co-operate in the recognition of their common interests, objectives and goals (Mitchell, 1987). In a sense, organisations use knowledge, techniques and resources in order to accomplish the task. In order to achieve this the organisation utilises certain general principles which were originally developed by the early sociologist Max Webber (1947) at the end of the last century, namely the notion of 'role', 'authority', 'harmony', 'status', 'bureau', and 'rationality' (Handy,

1985). It is not therefore unusual to see that organisations were assumed to be rational and logically structured and therefore it was thought that people within work organisations would also behave in a rational manner (Burrell and Morgan, 1979; Kakabadse, 1983).

Since the early days of the development of management the notions of 'order', 'predictability' and even 'rationality' itself have been challenged and questioned (Analoui, 1993). In short, the inseparable relationship between 'organisations' and 'management' theories have meant that management theories evolved, and were based, around the ways organisations were viewed (London, 1987).

From the 'traditional perspective', for example organisations were viewed as hard, easily definable entities which were mechanistically structured and were operating based on the scientific laws and general principles (Blau and Scott, 1966). People, therefore, were treated as components of a mechanical structure and were even described as the 'cogs' of a machine who were expected to behave in an orderly fashion in a predictable environment (Salaman, 1992). Management therefore was simply viewed as a science, the study of the dynamics of the forces within organisations which co-ordinates the activities of the sub-systems and relates them to the environment (Etzioni, 1964; Elliott et. al., 1990). Managers were needed to maximise the utilisation of resources in the most scientific and efficient ways.

The traditional perspective, not surprisingly, did not place the emphasis on 'people' and therefore paid more attention to 'task' at the expense of 'people' and their development. It ignored the need to recognise, for example, what Human Relations theorists refer to as the social system of the organisation, the community of people and their development of norms of behaviour and the presence of informal codes of conduct (McGregor, 1987). In this era, management was seen as the art of getting things done through people (Kakabadse, et. al., 1987) and therefore since people constituted the most important ingredient of the work organisation, managers required not only the skills for carrying out the task but also required the skills of dealing with people (Analoui, 1993).

Inevitably the human relations values, thoughts and beliefs were challenged by the 'open system' and the 'contingency philosophy' which emphasised on the need for flexibility in order to cope with changing markets and expectations (Drucker, 1988). It referred to immediate (contingent or touching) circumstances. Such a perspective treated individuals as those with the potential for development, learning and ultimately the capability of managing themselves. It is therefore not surprising to see that organisations to which the 'open system' managerial

3

principles have been applied and practised are defined as having tentative boundaries and with flexible relationships organised in a complex way (Katz and Khan, 1985). Such organisations, are comprised of sub-systems and they themselves are part of a bigger more complex system. They are being affected by changes in their environment and indeed they introduce change to their internal and external environments. Survival alone is no longer the focus of attention and the goal for managers with open system perspectives, but change and development have become the main concern (Kanter, 1984; 1989)

The parallel between development of organisational theories, the managers and perspectives in management and the underlying assumptions held by their advocates about people can be best shown below.

Development of Management Perspectives Within System Context

Assumptions		Perspectives	
Organisation	Closed system	Semi-open (modified)	Open system
People	Cogs of a mechanical Structure	Social agents of work community	Complex Socio-technical and information system
Approaches to Management	Classical management	Human relations	Contingency system

It is important to remember that each set of assumptions concerning the nature of the organisation, its principles and approaches to its management provided a basis for practices and procedures which over time became a domain of belief and values system. These sets of dominant values systems which are often referred to as schools of thought, encapsulated other approaches with their own prescriptions of 'right' and 'wrong' practices. However, the overall dominance of a set of distinguishable values, beliefs and thoughts remained dominant within the boundaries of each perspective.

Traditional perspective

A major attempt was made in the early days of this century by Taylor (1911) and his followers who saw the organisation as a hard, tangible mechanical system with a tendency for 'order' and 'harmony'. These assumptions were based on Webber's (1947) original conception of the nature of the organisation which was 'hierarchical', based on status quo and which advocated the relationship between authority and position within the hierarchy of the organisation (Gant, 1919; Gilberth, 1941). Thus the vague notion of so called Scientific Management emerged, one which became the foundation for the studies of organisational and management scholars, practitioners, planners and developers. It still remains a powerful and influential philosophy throughout the world, particularly within the third world countries and the newly formed transitional economies (Emerson, 1962; Fayol, 1916; Etzioni, 1964).

It is imperative to note that despite the numerous criticisms that it has faced, it still remains a dominant philosophy amongst those who believe in centralisation of planning, decision making and power within the organisation. Even within transition economies, its assumptions are nowadays being questioned and challenged by scholars, developers and practitioners. Management thinkers and writers therefore contributed the most to the growth and development of this school of thought. Their contributions will be briefly noted below.

Principles of management

The name Taylor (1911) is synonymous with the term 'scientific management'. It was the result of his studies conducted in the 'Bethlehem Steel Company' that provided a scientific basis for designing and measuring jobs. He believed that, by breaking down the elements of each task into a number of separate components and finding the most efficient way of working on those tasks, it is possible to increase productivity, generate economic rewards and ultimately achieve prosperity for both the organisation and the individuals. His main principles for management were;

Development of true science of work The scientific investigation of a daily task; work can then be planned and task is discharged under optimum conditions (Work Study).

Scientific selection and progressive development of the workmen Workers were selected to ensure that they possess physical and intellectual qualities to enable them to achieve the specified output systematically and each can be trained to be a 'first-class' man.

Bringing together of the science of work and scientifically selected and trained men providing mechanism in place to ensure the co-operation between men and management.

Constant and intimate co-operation of management and men By understanding each other's task and understanding who is best suited for what (psychological acceptance of status quo).

Underlying philosophy is that co-operation is an essential pre-condition for the implementation of scientific management and that co-operation can be substituted for conflict.

Taylor's belief was based on the assumption that science is the only solution (science means systematic observation and measurement and application of the generalised rules, principles and laws). Therefore, it was believed that once natural laws governing work and productivity are discovered, then everyone will adhere to the laws of the situation and there will be no place for conflict (Mooney and Reily, 1947).

Fayol (1916) was one of the earliest exponents of a general theory of administration. He defined administration in terms if five primary elements: planning, organisation, command, co-ordination and control These, later have become the foundation for considering the basic processes or functions of management. Fayol argued that managerial activity was the problem and solution for all organisations, for example, industrial, public services and churches.

His first analysis was to divide the activities in an industrial undertaking into six main groups. These were;

- Technical activities (production, manufacture, adaptation).
- Commercial activities (buying, selling, exchange).
- Financial activities (search for optimum use of capital).
- Security activities (protection of property and persons).
- Accounting activities (stocktaking, balance sheets, costs, statistics).
- Managerial activities (planning, organisation, command, co-ordination, control).

It was suggested that management answer to those activities are:

- Forecast and plan - essentially looking forward, deciding what is to be achieved by the organisation and planning to achieve those objectives.

6

- Organise - building up the structure, material and human resources of the undertaking.
- Command - maintaining activity amongst the personnel.
- Co-ordinate - binding together unifying and harmonising all activity and effort.
- Control - seeing that everything occurs in conformity with established rules and expressed command.

Another influential management writer, Urich, (1952) when discussing the 'Elements of Administration' separated the principle of forecasting from planning, thus presenting principles of management as six managerial activities.

Critique of traditional view

This approach to organisations and their management has been subject to substantial criticism (Bravaman, 1974). For example;

- It employs close system assumptions in order to reduce uncertainty and maximise control.
- Many of its principles are based on common sense 'Truism' and suffer from generality, in that they lack specific guidelines for applications.
- It regards the organisation as 'Machine' and people as its components, 'organisation without people'.
- At its best it regards the individuals as 'economic man', only motivated by money.

It, therefore, disregards the social and more complex needs of individuals in organisations. Nowadays, communication has been given more emphasis than ever before, however although analysis may differ in certain aspects, or maybe highlighted in one aspect more than others, nevertheless Fayol's work still represents a most useful framework in which management, in general, can be studied.

Despite the many criticisms, the classical approach still remains influential even today. Many of its principles have formed the foundation for the development of the modern management concepts.

Human relations school (semi-open system)

This movement began out of scientific management with industrial psychologist's attempting to devise ways to select and match the best person for the job. During the early part of the twentieth century, many industrial psychologists resorted to investigations in order to improve the relationships between the individuals and the work environment, hence increased productivity. Mayo (1945) and other researchers were interested in finding out whether people at work were operating at their full capacity; and how far their performance was affected by factors such as temperature, lighting, humidity and noise in the workshop. In a sense, there seemed to be an attempt on the part of the new theorists and writers to find ways of improving the quality of life in work organisations. This, it was believed, would increase the job satisfaction and productivity of employees as a result (Hackman and Suttle, 1977).

Hawthorn studies

Mayo (1945) and his colleagues carried out various experiments and realised that variables such as illumination and humidity cannot be treated separately from the meaning which individuals assign to them, their attitudes to them and pre-occupation with them. This led to studies on workers' morale, job satisfaction and work group cohesion. So workers were no longer perceived as an isolated physiological being, but as group members whose behaviour is controlled by group norms and values.

Major emphasis Major concepts about people, organisations and management.

- Organisations (work) have social systems as well as technical - economic system.
- The individual is not only motivated by economic incentives, but is motivated by diverse social and psychological factors.
- The informal work group became a dominant unit of consideration.
- 'Authoritarian' leadership patterns must be replaced by 'Democratic' styles.
- Increasing work satisfaction necessarily results in increased productivity and organisational effectiveness.
- Effective communication channels must be maintained between various levels of the hierarchy. Thus 'participation' must prevail.
- Management requires effective social skills as well as technical skills.

- Participants can be motivated in the organisation by fulfilling certain socio- psychological needs.

The work of the founders of human relations was started off, like many major works, by behavioural scientists.

Open system approach

System approaches, is believed to be able to unify many fields of knowledge, physics, biology, and social sciences, all as a broad frame reference.

Ackoff (1974) notes, 'A system is a whole that cannot be taken apart without loss of its essential characteristics, and hence it must be studied whole'. Now instead of explaining a whole in terms of its parts, parts began to be explained in terms of the whole.

The Open System view recognises the dynamic relationship with its environment and receives various inputs, transforms these inputs in some way, and exports outputs. These systems are open both 'internally' - between the subsystems - and 'externally' between the system and environment (Trist, 1963; Miller and Rice, 1967).

The organisation can be considered in terms of a general open system model, see model below:

Inputs	------>	Transformation	-------->	Outputs
<---------------		Feedback	<---------	

Figure 1 A simple organisation system

Source: Kakabadase et. al., 1987, p.34.

The open system is one which is in continual two- way interactions with its environment until it achieves a 'steady state' or dynamic equilibrium while still retaining the capacity for work or energy transformation. These are open not only in relation to their environment but also in relation to themselves, or 'internally' in that interactions between components affect the system as a whole (Mintzberg, 1973). The open system adapts to its environment by changing the structure and processes of its internal component. The system must receive sufficient input of resources to maintain its operation and also to export the transformed resources to the environment in sufficient quantity to continue the cycle (Kakabadse et. al., 1987; Stewarts, 1982).

As Appleby aptly asserts, 'The changing uncertain environment makes a manager's job complicated and difficult. What can be stated with reasonable certainty is that the higher a manager's position in an organisation, the more likely he or she will emphasise planning activities and be more concerned with external aspects rather than concentrate on daily operations and activities (1994, p. 35).

Human resource development and management

Assumptions and emphasis

Theory X and Y McGregor (1987) in his famous book, 'The Human Side of the Organisation', contrasted the classical approach to management and human relations. He argued that in order to understand the ways people (human resources) behaved and consequently were managed, two theories, namely X and Y need to be considered.

Theory X essentially is used by the followers of scientific management who assume people are lazy (avoid responsibility) and incapable of supervising their own activities. They dislike work and do not wish to take responsibility (Pugh, 1990). The solution preferred by the exponents of classical management is to use threats, and coercion or to motivate people by economic incentives and other material means to make them work. The assumption is since people are not capable of self management they ought to be fully controlled and supervised (Hickson and Pugh, 1989).

The followers of Theory Y believed in the principles of Human Relations School of thought, and suggested the opposite to the exponents of Theory X. They argued that people are basically interested in their job, like to take responsibility and are active and willing to undertake work. Therefore, management do not have to resort to 'carrot' and 'stick' as a means to manage people at work. People should be provided with meaningful jobs, one which offers satisfaction, responsibility and can contain elements of growth and development. Whilst the advocates of Theory X emphasised on 'control' the followers of Theory Y placed emphasis on the 'transitory nature of people' and the gradual move towards ensuring 'commitment' and self management.

10

Table 1.1

Aspects of HRM	Emphasis Classical Management (*Theory X*)	Differences Human Resource Management (*Theory Y*)
Job Design	Individual performance; De-skilling, breaking job to its basic elements Thinking and need for accountability	Group participation and need for problem solving in order to increase quality of working life
Organisation Structure and Managerial Style	Hierarchical with top down control system; need for rules and co- ordination status and authority related to position in hierarchy situation of organisation	Emphasis on style rather than principles of management; belief that groups can be harnessed to provide self control
Performance Expectation	Well defined standard and maximum performance; 'harmonised' work Placement is desired	Emphasis on 'order', 'harmony' others remain the same
Compensation Policies	Variable, individual pay, incentives, emphasis on cuts hourly pay	Compensation policies remain the same
Employment	Employees regarded as variable 'costs'	Participation will result in extra effort & avoiding 'lay off'
Employee Voice Policy	Employee voice allowed on narrow agenda	Addition of limited ad-hoc consultation and corporate mechanism remains the same
Employee - management Relationship	'Them' and 'us' emphasis Unitary interest	Emphasis on quality of life and employee involvement; pluralism of interest and common goal

Source: Walton, R. E. (1980), Establishing and Maintaining High Commitment Work Systems, in J. Kimberly and R. Moles (eds), The Organisational Life Cycle, Jossey - Bass, San Francisco.

11

Walton (1980) has appropriately compared the approaches or points of emphasis, in so far as the management of human resources is concerned by the followers of the above two management schools as follows.

Contingency and commitment With the emergence of open system thinking and the need to consider policy and procedures which are contingent upon the changing situation, explicit distinction was made between 'personnel management' and that of 'human resource management'.

Guest (1987) in his article, 'Human Resource Management and Industrial Relations', suggests that personnel management which has been adopted and preferred by the managers and officials who advocate to 'traditional' and 'human relations' principles, has been developed based on the short, ad hoc and closed rather than integrated and open system approach (see table below).

Table 1.2
Stereotypes of Personnel Management and Human Resource Management

	Personnel Management	Human Resource Management
Time and Planning Perspective	Short-term, reactive, ad hoc, marginal	Long-term, pro-active, strategic, integrated
Psychological Contract	Compliance	Commitment
Control Systems	External controls	Self-control
Employee-relations Perspective	Pluralist, collective, low-trust	Unitarist, individual, high trust
Preferred Structures/ Systems	Bureaucratic, mechanistic, centralised, formal defined roles	Organic devolved flexible, roles
Roles	Specialist/professional	Largely integrated into line management
Evaluation Criteria	Cost-minimisation	Maximum utilisation (human asset accounting)

Source: Guest. D, 'Human Resource Management and Industrial Relations', Journal of Management Studies, 24 (5), 1987, p.507.

Personnel vs. human resource management

Personnel Management (PM) is defined as activities 'directed at the organisation's employees and finding and training them, arranging for them to be paid, explaining management's expectations, justifying management's action, satisfying their needs, dealing with their problems, and seeking to modify management's actions that could produce an unfavourable response' (Storey, 1992, p.6). The position of PM could be best described as a middle ground position between the management and the employees. PM does place high priority on employees attitude, interests and responses (Guest, 1987). It is for this reason that personnel managers can not totally identify with the management and when able to do so they become quasi - representatives of the organisations' workforce.

The HRM on the other hand is directed not necessarily mainly at the needs of the employees but the whole human resource of the organisation. More emphasis is placed on the planning, monitoring and commitment than problem solving and mediation (Torrington, 1995). HRM covers the broad spectrum of the life of the employees at work; from entry to final exit. It is also argued that HRM is about human struggle for improved condition of service, management of career expectations, motivation, training and development, and it relates to the management of distributive justice in an organisation (Giwa, 1990). Handy (1985) also contends that HRM is about organisational development which is aimed at changing the culture of the organisation so that 'the goals and values of the individual and those of the organisational are integrated' (p.284).

Of course, there has also been a view that, HRM is basically 'nothing but a newly enriched name for PM' (Barkin, 1989, p.699). It has even been suggested that some companies have simply given their PM the new title of HRM, and that 'many find it difficult to distinguish between the two (Klatt et. al., 1989, p.104). Cowan (1988) argues that 'we should not continue to waste time and effort in debating whether we are engaged in HRM or PM ... that HRM and PM might be complementary' (p.36).

It is however, notable that as Armstrong (1988) suggests, HRM adopts a more strategic and far reaching approach as oppose to the position of the PM which is characterised by a less dynamic and short term view of the organisation and its needs. HRM is devoted to shaping an appropriate corporate culture by means of planned intervention such as introducing programmes which reflect and support the core values system of the enterprise (WHO, 1984).

There are three dimensions to HRM: maintenance or development; the operational and strategic; and personal and organisational growth

13

(Fomburan, et. al., 1984, p.4). Strategically, HRM identifies the broad substantive areas and emphasises the 'necessity for an appropriate linkage with the external competitive strategy of the individual organisation' (Salaman, 1992, p.23). Kiggundu (1989), contends that Human Resource Development (HRD) constitutes the 'development' dimension of the HRM. Thus, it relates to development of the institutional arrangement, and behavioural process for the acquisition of the knowledge, skills and abilities and values to bring about general improvements in human condition.

Basically, the major areas of differences between PM and HRM are as follows;

- PM is about administration and procedures while HRM is about strategic approach to acquisition, motivation and management of organisational human resources.
- HRM has adopted the executive roles and has transferred the PM to the level of line management. Not surprisingly, HR managers do adopt advisory roles as opposed to purely function and implementing roles.
- Personnel management is preoccupied with the day to day running of the organisation where as HRM assumes an advisory role and attempts to ensure that the organisational activities are closely linked with corporate strategy and that they fit the culture of the organisation (Handy, 1985).

In agreement with Armstrong (1992), it is suggested that HRM nowadays has graduated and matured from its 'transitory' state and thus ought to place more emphasis on 'commitment' on the part of their employees and employers rather than 'control' which is exercised by the employer alone. In this way, the individual employees and/or managers are expected to take responsibility for upgrading the system performance since the emphasis should be on job redesign, whole task, doing and thinking.

In a flat and leaner type of organisation structure with co-ordinating and controlling shared mechanism which is based on shared values and beliefs, teams are developed and utilised in order to achieve higher objectives. The whole affair should emphasise on flexibility of defining duties and orientation towards the need for contingency upon the changing market and business environment.

In organisations with less emphasis on hierarchical status and differentiation, the HRM will place emphasis on availability of information to all and reward system which is extended beyond individual pay towards orientation of equity, profit sharing, advancement and skills and mastery of work. Employees are provided with training and re-training with assurance that participation and commitment will not result in loss of employment. In such a new corporate governance environment the HRM policy will stress on the employees voice participation and a wider range of issues because it is believed that the employees as recipients of information will benefit from joining, participating in and contributing to meetings and other group and team related activities (Beaumont, 1993).

Theory Z

The unprecedented economic growth and development of Japan during the last few decades has drawn the attention of management theorists and specialists towards the ways in which Japanese organisations were organised and the ways in which they dealt with their employees and managed their human resources affairs at work (Nakane and Chie, 1973: Thong, G.1991). Ouchi (1981), in his work 'Theory Z' suggests that the success of the Japanese in comparison with contemporary American organisations is largely due to the adoption of human resources policies which encourage commitment, participation and as a result lead to innovation, better performance and flexibility to meet the changing needs of the market economy (see table below).

Table 1.3
Ouchi's Theory Z

Japanese organisations	American organisations
Life-time employment	Short-term employment
Slow evaluation and promotion	Rapid evaluation and promotion
Non-specialist career paths	Specialised career paths
Implicit control mechanisms	Explicit control mechanisms
Collective decision-making	Individual decision-making
Collective responsibility	Individual responsibility
Holistic concern	Segmented concern

Source: Adapted from Ouchi (1981), Theory Z, Addison Wesley, Reading, Mass.

It is believed that the culture of the Theory Z and Japanese management provides the soft and flexible environment which is suitable for the growth of the HRM (Sethi, et. al., 1984). However, concern has been raised as to whether such characteristics are unique and specific to Japan or are universally applicable. Many refer to the duality of this debate and suggest that the followers of the rationalist school argue that the roots of HRM practices in Japanese firms lie in rational responses to industrial development and are therefore, universally applicable (Kono, 1992; Dedoussis, 1995).

The followers of the culturalist school of thought, argue that the Japanese management is reflective of Japanese traditions and thus unique to Japan' (Beechler and Yang, 1994, p.469). Whether, theory Z is visible to outsiders or not, it is deeply rooted in Japanese specific social and cultural values and the system is sustained and supported by Japanese psychological attachment to it. Kono suggests that management practices in, for example, educational systems, which are related to a deep core of cultural values such as environmental characteristics, are hard to transfer' (1992, p.22).

Theory Z has been successfully adapted by some American companies and other Japanese overseas subsidiaries, especially, in South- east Asia. They have successfully introduced some aspects of the Theory Z's element in to the HRM strategic polices and practices in the organisation. However, there is the view that because of the bureaucratic nature of the organisations within Less Developed Countries and Economies and the fact that the management of these organisations favour values and beliefs of classical management, it would be difficult to introduce principles of the Theory Z and indeed, a meaningful system of HRM into these organisations. The difficulty is partly due to the static and hierarchical nature of the organisations, especially within the public sector, a generally lower level of education, less developed institutions and a lack of incentive and motivation on the part of the human resource (employees and employers) to accept new values and beliefs which may not have cultural supports for their realisations.

Conclusion

The development of the management to date is marked with the emergence of the dominant values systems to which many theorists, writers and practitioners have subscribed. Each perspective is built upon a set of assumptions which in turn determine the ways human resources in organisations are viewed, dealt with and ultimately managed.

Theories X, Y and Z offer insight into the ways managers typically deal with human resources at work. The policies and procedures adopted by the

PM and HRM specialists reflects the above concerns and belief systems. Whilst, it would seem feasible to emulate one system in many organisations, managers are warned that inadequate emphasis placed on the unique 'culture' of the organisation may result in failure to manage its human resource effectively.

To develop human resources at work, managers ought to pay attention to the nature of the complex relationships amongst and between the subsystems of their organisation, and their organisation and other influential external forces in their market. Managers ought to understand that their HRM and HRD policies and procedures should be made contingent upon the circumstances in which they find themselves, often without prior warning.

References

Ackoff, R. (1974), *The Systems Age*, Wiley, New York.

Analoui, F. (1993), 'Skills of Management' in *Management of the Projects with Developing Countries*, Chapter Five, Edited by J. Cusworth and T. Franks, Longman, Scientific and Technical.

Armstrong, M. (1992), *A Hand Book of Human Resource,* Kogan Page, London.

Barkin, S. (1989), 'Human Resource Management Examine Itself and Its Limitations', *Relations Industrielles*, vol. 6, no. 1, pp.1-14.

Beechler, S. And Yang, J. (1994), 'The Transfer of Japanese - style of Management to American Subsidiaries: Contingencies, Constraints and Competencies', *Journal of International Business Studies*, vol. 25, no.3, pp.467-90.

Beaumont, P.B. (1993), *Human Resource Management: Key Concepts and Skills*, Sage Publication, London.

Blau, P. M. and Scott, W. R. (1966), *Formal Organisations*, Routledge and Kegan Paul.

Bravaman, H.(1974), Labour and Monopoly Capital, Monthly Review Press.

Burrell, G. and Morgan, G. (1979), *Sociological Paradigms and Organisation Analysis*, Arena Publishing Company, England.

Cowan, A. (1988), *Quality for the Manager*, Common Wealth and Industrial Library of Social administration Training economics and Production Division, Oxford, London.

Dedoussis, V. (1995), 'Simply a Question of Cultural Barriers: The search for New Perspectives in the Transfer of Japanese Management Practices', *Journal of Management Studies*, vol, 32, no.6, pp.731-45.

Drucker, P. F. (1988), *The Effective Executive*, William Heinemann, Paperback Edition.

Elliott, R. D. (1990), 'The Challenge of Managing Change', *Personnel Journal*, vol. 69, no.3. March.

Emerson, R. M. (1962), 'Power-Dependence Relations', *American Sociological Review*, vol. 1., no. 27., pp.25-40.

Etzioni, A. (1964), *Modern organisations*, Prentice-Hall, p.41.

Fomburan, C. (1984), *Strategic Human Resource Management*, John Wiley and Sons.

Etzioni, A. (1964), *Modern Organisation*, Prentice - Hall.

Fayol, H. (1916), *Administration Undustrialelle et Generale*, Dunod, Paris.

Gant, H. L. (1919), 'Work, Wages and Profit', *Engineering Magazine Company*, New York.

Gilberth, F. L. (1941), *Motion Study*, Van Nostrad, New York.

Gima, R. F. (1990), 'Human Resource Management in 1990s: Prospects and Challenges', *Nigerian Journal of Personnel*, vol. 4, no. 1., pp.503-521.

Guest, E. D (1987), 'Human Resource Management and Industrial Relations', *Journal of Management Studies*, 2 4 (5), p.507

Handy, C. (1985), *Understanding Organisations*, Penguin, Business Publication.

Hickson, D. J. and Pugh, D. S. (1989), *Writers of Organisations*, (4th ed.), Penguin Books, London.

Kakabadse, A. P. (1983), *The Politics of Management*, Gower; Nichols Publishing Co., New York.

Kakabadse, A. Ludlow, R. and Vinnicombe, S. (1987), *Working In Organisations*, Penguin Books.

Kanter, R. M. (1984), *Change Masters*, Allen and Unwin, London.

Kanter, R. M. (1989), *When Giants Learn to Dance*, Simon and Schuster, London.

Kast, W.L.; Rosenweig, J.E. (1985), *Understanding Human Behaviour in Organisations*, Penguin, London.

Kiggundo, M. (1989), *Managing Organisations in Developing Countries*, Kumarian Press Inc., Texas, USA.

Klatt, A. L., Murdic, G. R., Schuster, E. S. (1989), *Human Resource Management*, Charles, E. Merrill Publishing Company, Ohio, USA.

18

Kono, T. (1992), 'Japanese Management Philosophy: can it be Exported', in Kono, H. (ed.), *Strategic Management in Japanese Companies*, Pergammon Press, Oxford.

London, K, (1978), *The People Side of the System*, McGraw Hill.

Mayo, E. (1945), *The Social Problems of the Industrial Civilisation*, Harvard University Press.

Mitchell, T. R. (1987), *People in Organisation: An introduction to organisational behaviour*, (3rd ed.), McGraw Hill Book Company, New York.

McGregor, D. (1987), *The Human Side of the Enterprise*, Penguin, New York.

Mintzberg, H. (1973), *The Nature of the Managerial Work*, Harper and Row, USA.

Mooney, J. D., Reily, A. C. (1947), *The Principles of Organisation*, Harper and Row, USA.

Nakane, C. (1973), *Japanese Society, Penguin Books*, Middlesex, England.

Ouchi, W. (1981), *Theory Z*, Addison Wesley, Reading, Mass., USA.

Pugh, S. (1990), *Organisation Theory*, (3rd ed.), Penguin Books., (ed.), Middlesex.

Salaman, G. (1992), *Human Resource Strategies*, (ed.), Sage, London.

Sethi, S., Namiki, N. And Swanson, C. (1984), *The False Promise of Japanese Miracle*, Pitman, London.

Silverman, D. (1970), *The Theory of Organisations*, Heinemann, London.

Stewarts, R. (1982), *Choices for the Managers: A Guide to Managerial Work*, McGraw Hill.

Storey, J. (1992), 'Human Resource Management in the Public Sector', in Salaman, G. (ed.). *Human Resource Strategies*, Sage, London.

Taylor, F.W. (1916), *The Principle of Scientific Management*, Harper and Row.

Thong, G. (1991), 'Foundation of Human Resource Practice in Japanese Companies in Malaysia', in Yamashita, S. (ed.) (1991), *Transfer of Japanese Technology and Management to ASEAN Countries*, University. of Tokyo Press, Tokyo, pp.135-49.

Torrington, D. And Hall, L., (1995), *Personnel Management:, HRM in Action*, (3rd Edition), Prentice Hall, London.

Trist, E. L. (1963), *Organisational Choice*, Tavistock Publications.

Urwick, L. (1952), *Notes on the Theory of Organisations*, American Management Association.

Walton, R. E. (1980), 'Establishing and Maintaining High Commitment Work Systems', in J. Kimberly and R. Moles (eds), *The Organisational Life Cycle*, Jossey - Bass, San Francisco.

Webber, M. (1947), *The Theory of Socio - economic Organisations*, Translated by: M. Henderson, and T. Glance, Parsons III, Free Press.

Miller, E. J., and Rice, A. K. (1967), *Systems of Organisation*, Tavistock Publications, UK.

World Health Organisations, (1984), *Human Resource Development*, Division of Environmental Health, WHO, 1121, Geneva.

2 Just like home but at work: gendered negotiation in private and public domains

Oriel Kenny

Introduction

In recent years there has been a shift away from discussing women in development to a focus on gender and development: this is partly due to recognition of the need also to study men if the power relations between men and women are to be changed for the better (Sweetman, 1997). Focussing on women alone, apart from the tendency to overburden women with more work in addition to their existing responsibilities, misses the vital issue of the necessary interaction and negotiation between the sexes in our daily lives: at home, in the community, at work and in public life. Much has been learned about womens gender identities and roles in recent years (as an antidote to previous work which was perceived as 'gender blind') but there has been little examination of mens' gender identities in development research although it is quite well developed in other disciplines. This chapter will consider the extent to which social conditioning affects womens' participation in the home, the community and beyond and suggest that a fuller examination of mens' gender interests is needed in order to facilitate meaningfull gender equity.

Gender identities in the household

The capacity of women to be involved in participatory processes and life outside the home generally is affected by their socialisation. The emphasis today on public participation presupposes a capacity and willingness to engage in negotiation and debate, for example throughout the development planning process. However, since many women are effectively excluded from real decision-making in their home life, the reality is that women may choose to withdraw from the opportunity to be involved in participatory processes (Moser, 1993). Womens' background and experience also affects their ability to take up employment and, once employed, may limit their possibilities for advancement.

There is a need to look inside the household to trace how this has arisen. From an early age, children learn the gendered dimension of work and responsibilities which they must adhere to. The adults and older children who consciously and unconsciously influence them also reinforce their own learning in the process (Papanek, 1990, p.163). This 'socialization for gender inequality' is usually very successful particularly since the disadvantaged group, by not perceiving their disadvantage, themselves help to perpetuate those disadvantages (Kynch and Sen, 1983). If women appear content this is due to an unreflective view of their circumstances -with full knowledge of all aspects of their situation they would prefer to have their husbands' advantages (Annas, 1993). In the household, women often have little control over resources but at the same time generally have heavy commitments to meet others' needs (O'Neill, 1993). The management of household resources, including labour and income, impacts upon the way the household is organised and the roles and obligations of family members (Moore, 1994). Paradoxically, many societies accord high respect to mothers while at the same time conferring very little power upon women. Interestingly, several studies have shown that the households of lone female parents do not operate the same divisions of tasks by gender and boys from these households develop more open attitudes towards the division of labour and a greater sense of family responsibility (Chant, 1997). The household division of labour, while differing according to culture, usually ascribes work of lower status and lower remuneration (or unpaid) to women. The continued performance of certain tasks, supposedly allocated on the basis of 'natural' aptitudes, in fact leads men and women to acquire these different capabilities through repeatedly carrying out the activity (Kabeer, 1994). We are then identified with the type of work we do and our work defines us in society. The amount of work and output for which women are responsible is becoming more recognised, for example in agriculture, due to several in-depth case studies even though it is not yet fully reflected in official statistics. Therefore, if the value of womens' work was measured according to their indispensability to the household, it should be very high. That it is not so indicates a distinct difference between the actual and perceived value of work. Reproductive work, in the sense of reproduction of the household, is mainly womens' work and is low status. Yet, objectively, how can it be unproductive to nurture current and future workers when this support clearly contributes to output? The answer is that it is perceived as such and perceptions are an important influence on actual status and outcomes (Sen, 1987). A study of women lace workers in India

(Mies, 1982) revealed that women themselves also undervalue their work even when it is obviously productive although, significantly, the women in the study did not receive the income for their work.

The link between income and work value is most important in its effect on decision-making power. The division between paid and unpaid work leads to a biased perception of who 'produces', and who 'earns' what - hence the inferior economic position of many women (Sen, 1987). The bias relates to direct money earning even where women expend much time. Outside earnings are important in creating gender differentials in the family - the disparity is sharper where women have less outside earnings (Boserup, 1970). There is evidence that as women earn more income so their input to household decision-making increases. In Zambia it is acknowledged that if a man cannot finish paying the full brideprice then this 'debt' to his in-laws reduces his bargaining power in the household (Pottier, 1994). This can lead to renegotiation of gender relations as the basis of a more equitable sharing of decision-making power within the household but can lead to conflict. Research in Latin America (Kaztman, 1992) showed that men of lower status in the world of employment were most resistant to change at home and most keen to retain their dominant position in the family. If circumstances call the man's role as breadwinner into question, men may opt out of their traditional role or resort to violence neither of which are the desired outcomes. If co-operation breaks down under economic stress men are more likely to leave the household when the cost of maintaining dependents is perceived as too high.

It has been observed that womens' dependent status arises less from their confinement to the domestic sphere - and the boundaries between the home and the world are contested anyway - than from their lack of control over resources including the product of their own labour (Leacock, 1978). Womens dependence on men is expressed very clearly in relation to money: monetary transactions are often entirely in the male domain and it may be considered disrespectfull to ask for money even though womens need for money can be a source of constant conflict. Indeed, women often strive to obtain money through extra income earning activities in order to avoid asking their husbands. Men may approve of their wives' income earning activities but only while the amount of money earned is small and so unlikely to upset the balance of power in the household.

There is a considerable difference in household power relations depending on whether household finances are pooled or whether the household has a common purse. Thus, one would expect to find considerable difference between for example, West Africa and South Asia. A separate purse can be the key to greater autonomy for women giving greater access to resources both within and outside the household as well as separate spheres of influence. In recent research in Cameroon (Jones, 1995) it was observed that women spend long hours on their own fields to an extent that could not be explained in terms of returns to labour. It is because they control the output and so suggests that this is a way of women creating 'space' for themselves. Work on their husbands' fields was less attractive and entailed negotiation regarding working conditions and remuneration. The question then arises whether men are likely to be more co-operative or less so if women have more economic power or does it give more scope for conflict? In Cameroon, frequent and pronounced conflict occurred between men and women regarding division of income from rice production because each want to use the money in different ways. This raises the question of whether there would be less conflict where men have all the power in the household and women perceive their best strategy to be passive and seek access to decision making through their sons? More corporately organised households, for example in the Indian sub-continent, exhibit little overt conflict over household decision-making: mens total control over resources is such that womens' best strategy is often to acquiesce and even perpetuate the existing system (Kabeer, 1994).

The nature of conflict of interest within a household is quite different to other conflicts mainly because the protagonists live together and so should benefit from co-operation. Although serious conflicts of interest exist, the nature of the family unit make it necessary to adopt generally co-operative strategies for the good of the household. Thus, there are repeated opportunities for co-operation or conflict over the arrangement of the household, that is who does or who gets what. Sen (1987) refers to this as the bargaining problem: although it is assumed that collusion is better for both (or all) parties, the actual outcome depends on relative bargaining power. If they cannot co-operate there is the possibility of breakdown occurring and womens breakdown position is seen to be worse than mens because they are less able to secure an outcome favourable to them and would suffer more from breakdown of the family unit. 'A woman who has no adequate entitlements of her own, and insecure rights to a share in family property or income ... is always vulnerable to coercion' (O'Neill, 1993 p.320). Also, the outcome of one 'bargaining episode' influences future bargaining power. For example, mens' better education and greater freedom to work outside the home, together with the skills so gained, makes their future bargaining position stronger. Some men use their greater bargaining power within the household to renegotiate the distribution of responsibilities in their favour (Moore, 1994). Womens negotiating position is weaker because:

1. Pregnancy and childbirth lowers womens ability to make a perceived economic contribution to the household.

2. Since adult women have had less education and other opportunities they are usually able to earn less and have less secure employment opportunities should the family unit break down. Women also face discrimination in access to land, capital and credit. Hence, women are much worse off economically in case of total breakdown and most societies also operate social sanctions against lone or divorced women.
3. Women are often said not to have a notion of personal well-being separate from that of the family and being therefore disinclined to value their interests above those of the household they will concede first.

Gender identities in the workplace

It has been said that schools reinforce and further the differentiation between boys and girls which starts in the home. Although there is now mostly equal access to the full range of subjects, more subtle discriminations persist' for example in boys' command of playground space and of teachers attention (Spender, 1982). A study of careers advice in the UK (Stanworth, 1983) illustrated how personal biases affected the advice given: when asked to predict what pupils would go on to do, even the brightest girls were envisaged in subordinate, supportive roles. In contrast boys, regardless of ability, were seen in jobs with responsibility and authority. It is therefore not surprising that a boy and girl of comparable ability would find themselves located very differently in employment. The employment circumstances of women and men are significantly shaped by their prior socialisation: gender identities learned at home and school carry over into our work and public life and decree that men and women do not compete in the labour market on an equal basis.

Their status in the household will affect womens' ability to participate outside the home and for many women the reality is that their main connection to the wider world is through the males of their household. How then does social conditioning affect women at work? Women in subordinate positions will obviously have less negotiating power than senior men but it is often the case that women of equal work status also have less negotiating power in the workplace than their male peers. Again, perception is all important. As we carry over our home roles, women are more likely to volunteer to make the tea or take minutes in a meeting but, more importantly, their male colleagues will expect them to! This is understandable in that both men and women are used to women's subordinate position in the family. Thus the pattern becomes self perpetuating. Since women are universally responsible for the 'Second Shift' that is, maintaining the household (whether or not they are in paid employment) the image of womens' subordinate position in the household follows her to work both in her own mind and in the perception of male colleagues. Mens' ability to appropriate womens' unpaid physical and emotional labour (Pateman, 1988) not only frees them to focus solely on paid work but can influence their impression of womens' engagement with their paid work. Progress to senior positions in an organisation generally depends upon 'evaluations' which are ostensibly gender neutral. Given the employee profile of most organisations these are in practice mostly the responsibility of men who therefore reproduce men's dominance and frame women as less valued and less worthy of higher status (Martin, 1996).

Many countries now enshrine the concept of equal opportunities for all citizens in their constitutions and organisations - notably the civil service - often go beyond the brief definition in law in an attempt to provide meaningful equal opportunities in the workplace. However, policy statements and even clearly defined practical measures designed to work towards real equality of opportunity must be viewed in the context of prevailing social structures and existing gender inequalities in the workplace. Men, for example, have generally defended gender-linked pay differentials even concerning their wives in order to maintain their position as the breadwinner (White, 1994). Where there are predominantly male staff at senior levels, organisations may not even follow their own policy regarding gender equity. It has been said that there is no need for active discrimination against women when the culture of an organisation can be relied upon to reproduce the status quo (The Observer, 1996). Furthermore, as noted above, women as well as men bring their social conditioning to work and hence do not always readily take action to demand the application of their existing rights. Following this reasoning, it may be sufficient to adopt a genuinely gender neutral position, rather than being actively pro woman, in order to significantly improve womens position.

Some work on negotiation in the workplace, for example the Harvard Model, contrasts 'hard' and 'soft' bargaining positions in the workplace - while it is presumably intended to be gender neutral, it could be approximated to male/female strategies for negotiation - and suggests 'negotiating on the merits' to encourage a fair and equitable outcome (Fisher and Ury, 1987). This involves focussing on the issue rather than the people and basing the outcome on objective criteria rather than relative power. The implications for training, recognising that it is not a question of womens' ability/aptitude but of our perceptions of men and women, are that assertiveness should not only concern shifting women from being passive to being assertive but perhaps also to shift men from being aggressive to being assertive. Gender sensitivity is necessary for both women and men, but unfortunately it has been assumed to concern only women for too long. The question arises whether women and men should train together on these issues - probably the majority of women feel gender training should be segregated partly due to fears that men would dominate the proceedings. This is perhaps based on their school experience of gender discrimination in use of space and access to teachers' attention, since studies have shown that both men and women teachers discriminate in favour of boys because they command attention (Spender, 1982). At senior levels of organisations, however, it is generally acknowledged that gender becomes a much less significant factor and mixed training would be more appropriate.

Strategies to redress past gender inequality with recognition of womens contributions and needs have made women more visible but the effect has often been the identification of women as a 'problem' or at best peripheral to the mainstream. However, policy usually has little if anything to say about how women can take up new opportunities and become more productive if they cannot redistribute their domestic responsibilities beyond female family members: across all classes and cultures the division of unpaid, time consuming household work remains one-sided. Even where men (and sometimes women) perceive that domestic tasks are shared equitably it is not found to be the reality and raises the issue again of gendered assumptions (Hochschild, 1989). While it is acknowledged that women have entered many new work roles, men have not made a corresponding move into the sphere of domestic and caring work for so long viewed as womens' realm (Dunne, 1997). This issue is relevant to all sectors of the workforce: although the problems of higher status women balancing the home/work interface are probably the best known, this cohort also has more resources to alleviate the situation. What ever resources women may command to deal with the logistical problems of 'juggling', the fact that it remains womens' responsibility reinforces our impression of the different spheres of operation/influence of men and women. Attempts to provide services such as nurseries often founder due to the cost of services which women are generally expected to fulfill without payment.

Conclusion

The structure of the family and the definition of individuals' roles within it is changing. There is an increasing proportion of female headed households at least de facto - in some cases related to family life cycles and optimal labour use - and so many women have had to take on traditionally male roles. Renegotiation of roles and responsibilities is then necessary if the absent spouse returns. With economic and hence work uncertainties, the opportunities for conjugal conflict and negotiation over income and household decision-making have increased. Womens' identities now encompass their workplace status as well as more traditional spheres whereas it seems that mens' identities have not similarly widened to incorporate their non workplace identities. As women enter paid work their enhanced status as workers, as well as their economic contribution to the household, might raise their aspirations for more equitable negotiation over distribution of decision-making power in the home. However, the reality of lower wage and work status vis a vis her husband or male peers, as well as her vulnerable breakdown position, reduces womens' hopes and aspirations (Hochschild, 1989). This overlap between private and public lives must be recognised if the intention is to achieve real equity and empowerment. It is clearly inadequate to treat gender as purely a womens' issue if we hope to achieve real change. A way needs to be found to enable both women and men to work together towards a more equitable future. This will include making men an issue in gender work and incorporation of this approach into development practice.

References

Adepoju, A and Oppong, C (1994), *Gender, Work and Population in Sub-Saharan Africa*, (eds) ILO/James Curry/Heinemann.

Annas, J (1993), 'Women and the quality of life: two norms or one?' in Nussbaum, M and Sen, A (eds), *The Quality of Life*, Clarendon, Oxford.

Boserup, E (1970), *Womens Role in Economic Development*, London.

Casinader, R.A. et. al. (1987), 'Women's issues and men's roles: Sri Lankan village experience', in Momsen, J.H. and Townsend, J (eds) *Geography of Gender*, Hutchinson.

Chant, S (1997), *Women Headed Households*, Macmillan.

Dunne, G A (1997), 'Why Can't a Man Be More Like A Woman? in search of balanced domestic and employment lives', *LSE Gender Institute Discussion Paper*, issue 3.

Fisher, R and Ury, W (1987), *Getting to Yes*, Arrow Books Limited, London.

Hochschild, A (1989), *The Second Shift*, Piatkus, London.

Jones, C W (1985), 'The mobilization of womens labor for cash crop production: a game theoretic approach' quoted in Kabeer, N (1994) *Reversed Realities: gender hierarchies in development thought*. Verso, London.

Kabeer, N (1994), *Reversed Realities: gender hierarchies in development thought*, Verso, London.

Kaztman, R (1992), Why are men so irresponsible?, *Cepal Review*. no.46.

Kynch, J and Sen, A (1983), 'Indian Women; Well-being and Survival' *Cambridge Journal of Economics*, no.7, pp.363-380.

Leacock, E (1978), Womens status in egalitarian society: implications for social evolution, *Current Anthropology,* vol 19, no.2, pp.247-275.

Martin, P Y (1996), Gendering and Evaluating Dynamics: Men, Masculinities and Management in Collinson, D L and Hearn, J (1996) *Men as Managers, Managers as Men,* Sage, London.

Mies, M (1982), *The Lace-makers of Narsapur: Indian housewives produce for the world market,* London, Zed.

Moore, H (1994), *Is there a crisis in the family?* Occasional paper no.3, World Summit for Social Development, UNRISD, Geneva.

Moser, C (1993), *Gender Planning and Development: theory, practice and training,* London, Routledge.

Nussbaum, M C and Sen, A (1993), *The Quality of Life Oxford,* Clarendon.

Observer (1996), February 11th.

O'Neill, O (1993), 'Justice, Gender, International Boundaries' in Nussbaum, M and Sen, A, *The Quality of Life Oxford,* Clarendon.

Papanek, H (1990), 'To Each Less Than She Needs, From Each More Than She Can Do: Allocations, Entitlements and Value' in Tinker, I (ed.) *Persistent Inequalities: women and world development,* OUP.

Pateman, C (1988), *The Sexual Contract,* Cambridge: Polity.

Pottier, J (1994), 'Poor Men, Intra-Household Bargaining and the Politics of household Food Security' in Yngstrom (ed.) *Gender and Environment in Africa,* University of Edinburgh Centre of African Studies Seminar Proceedings no. 32.

Sen, A (1987), *Gender and Co-operative Conflicts* WIDER working paper no 18.

Spender, D (1982), 'The role of Teachers: what choices do they have?' in Council of Europe (ed.), *Sex Stereotyping in Schools,* Zwets and Zeitlinger.

Stanworth, M (1983), *Gender and Schooling: a study of sexual divisions in the classroom,* London, Hutchinson.

Sweetman, C (ed.) (1997), 'Editorial-Men and Masculinity', *Gender and Development* 5(2).

Warner, M W et. al., (1997), 'Beyond Gender Roles? Conceptualizing the Social and Economic Lives of Rural Peoples', in *Sub-Saharan Africa Development and Change,* 28:1, pp.143-168.

White, S (1994), 'Making Men an Issue' in MacDonald, M (ed.), *Gender Planning in Development Agencies: meeting the challenge.* Oxford: Oxfam.

3 Career development: a case study of managerial women in the Ghanaian Civil Service

Pauline M. Amos-Wilson

Introduction: women in the Ghanain Civil Service

Although only 16 per cent of Ghana's population of 15 million are in waged employment, 60 per cent of these work in the public sector. Within the public sector 25 per cent of employees are women. This is a small number perhaps but even in the current environment of structural adjustment programmes, wage freezes, and labour retrenchment, employment in the public sector represents a relatively secure career for women, when considered against the limited opportunities available. More than 90 per cent of women in Ghana are either self-employed, or unpaid farm labour. As part of the public sector the Civil Service is also an employer of women, but it is the workplace of a very small minority, who generally find themselves in junior positions operating in a predominantly male environment despite the fact that the first woman entered the Ghanaian Civil Service in 1890.

By the 1930s women constituted 8 per cent of public servants, in 1954 they were admitted to the executive class and finally in 1963 they were enabled to enter the top cadre, the administrative class (Harlley, 1995).

As in many other countries although women are represented in some numbers in the lower grades of the Civil Service, the top jobs are predominantly held by men. Table 3.1 indicates the gender distribution of the top four grades in 1995, when the study reported here was conducted.

Despite the apparent opportunity for women since 1963 to enter the most senior roles in public life, a mass breakthrough of what is frequently termed the 'glass ceiling', that is access to the most senior jobs of all, making policy and managing the Civil Service, seems elusive as ever for women. Questions must be posed as to why this should be the case. It cannot be argued that this effect is merely an accident of history. The period that has elapsed since 1963 is long enough to encompass an individual's entry into the profession, and their life of public service to very near retirement. This must be the case for very many men in senior grades in the Civil Service, yet there are so few women, even though as was discovered in the research reported below, many had been public servants all their working lives.

Table 3.1
Gender distribution in the top four grades of the
Ghanian Civil Service in 1995

Grade	Men	Women	Total
Minister	17	3	20
Deputy Minister	30	4	34
Chief Directors	15	0	15
Directors	138	15	153
Totals	200	22	222

Throughout the world, in academic and general literature, governmental reports, popular journals, news articles and the media, the reasons for women's lack of progression to top jobs are well rehearsed, this is not simply a phenomenon in Ghana (see for example The Hansard Society, 1990; Gellejeh, 1990; Wilson, 1991; Jemerigbe 1992; Khan, 1992; Turner and O'Connor, 1994).

The cited reasons usually include availability of suitable work, career breaks, the organisation of work which makes balancing of family and work demands problematic, and discrimination against women.

In this chapter specific aspects of women's career progression in managerial grades, choices, opportunities and behaviour will be investigated. The position that women find themselves in whilst creating, developing, confining and constraining their careers will be considered. It is claimed that these processes start early in life, continue throughout it, and interact with the attitudes of those in positions of power within organisations that control and influence women's work opportunities in managerial jobs.

Since the prime interest is in identifying what factors might contribute to women's work role identifications and decisions. The data concerning the careers of a number of women civil servants in supervisory and managerial roles in Ghana will be examined. These data were collected as part of a larger study concerned with the status, position and role of women in the Civil Service in Ghana[1] (not reported here).

Although a number of factors contribute towards attitudes to women at work, and the behaviours women display, here a search for, and considerations of, only those which seem to impinge on women's interpretations of the roles and behaviours available to them will be included.

However, the discriminatory effects which are very considerable are not ignored, but the dynamics relating to the woman at the centre are looked at. In so doing, it is hoped to elicit some concepts or a model which can contribute to an understanding of the processes and factors involved. This understanding could, in turn, have implications for policy, for action and for training.

About the research

The data, in qualitative form, was collected by a team of four researchers during July and August 1995, from 62 women who were employed in the central Civil Service in Accra, Ghana. Semi-structured interviews were conducted and the life-career progress of participants reviewed. All but three interviews were tape recorded and transcriptions were made of 54 recordings. In addition notes were made during the interviews, and coding sheets were used to note simple data for descriptive statistical information.

Each of the two lead researchers independently applied a qualitative analysis to the data, for differing purposes. One concentrated on the production of a report concerned with the main purposes of the Department for International Development (DFID)[2] funded Women in Public Life (WIPL) project, to provide information for the public domain about the role, status and position of women in public life in Ghana and consequently to develop appropriate training programmes. The author considered the processes that occur in the development of career choice and career behaviour among managerial women civil servants and the implications of this. It is this aspect of the study which is reported here.

In taking part in the semi-structured interviews the women were in many cases reviewing their life histories. Although attempting to gain answers to a series of questions formulated for the interview the researchers did not intervene if the interviewee expanded beyond what was being asked. Useful prompts employed if the participant became stuck in her narrative included such phrases as 'tell me about your early life', or 'what happened then, or next'. No comments were made on the material, or attempts at categorisation with the individual, during the recording.

An appreciation of the issues, methods and techniques of qualitative research is a fundamental aspect of the validity of this study.

Qualitative research is not simply the gathering and analysis of non-numeric data, but issues of research practice and research ethics are also encompassed by it, and these have their roots in differing philosophical orientations to the nature and interpretation of knowledge. These orientations can be characterised as polar opposites which have variously been termed on the one side as 'positivist', 'hypothetico-deductive' or 'experimental' and on the other as 'naturalistic', 'discriptive' or 'contextual'.

It is the positivist, hypothetico-deductive approach, generated first in the natural sciences that has been the core of social science research. In this approach the tendency is to demonstrate causal relationships between the variables under scrutiny and demand control of variables and the testing of a stated theory.

However there has been a long history of critique of such an approach to the social domain, dating from the nineteenth century (see for example Droysen, 1858; Cicourel 1964; Dilthey, 1977; Geertz 1973; Denzin and Lincoln 1994). The emphasis of this alternative approach is on interpretation and understanding, not least through recognising the importance of attributed meaning. It is a constructivist approach, emphasising description, reflecting reality as perceived by participants of research, and insisting that an appreciation of both the context and internal complexities of experience and behaviour be incorporated in analysis of data. As such this approach is working towards the possible generation of hypotheses and concepts, rather than seeking to verify or falsify a prior theory.

The debate about qualitative versus quantitative data takes place against a backdrop of what constitutes 'proper knowledge'. There has been dissatisfaction with knowledge acquired in the past by quantitative methods, that it has not reflected truth as individuals know it, and the reality of their lives. (Woolgar, 1996; Bulmer, 1979; Hammersley, 1996; Silverman, 1993, Potter and Wetherall, 1988; Burman and Parker, 1993).

Feminist researchers also tend to reject traditional quantitative methods (Harding, 1986, 1987, 1991; Griffin 1995; Stanley and Wise 1983). Qualitative methods are frequently seen by feminist researchers as better able to reflect women's experiences in particular and with respect to this study I hold this viewpoint.

In assessing the quality of qualitative research it is also essential to remember an underlying paradigm, that is, it does not rest on notions of objectivity which split the researcher or analyst off from a knowable ultimate truth. The 'knower' takes part in the construction of the 'known'. This is recognised as a fact of qualitative research and is definitely not seen as a problematic of researcher bias.

The theoretical positions I adopted in approaching this investigation are as follows:-

- career development is one part of total life development,
- the position and status of women in management in the civil service in Ghana are mediated by the decisions made about them by those with power over career development,
- others' behaviours are instrumental in the structure of opportunity available,
- promotion in career is predicated on perceived effective or 'good' managerial behaviour which in turn is predicated upon understanding of prescriptions for best practise, largely generated by western-centric management theories and transmitted education,
- such management theories are, generally speaking, patriarchal, and alternative forms of practise are seen as 'not-management'.

Thus women's actions and self-created management identity, as they progress in their careers in organisations are not just a function of their sex genes, but are conditioned by a number of other factors, which include power relationships and beliefs about managerial behaviour held by women themselves and those around them. These factors are part of an individual's total life progression. Work career and the rest of life interact with each other.

Although the aims of qualitative research include the understanding of the phenomena under investigation and the methods tend to elicit a large amount of rich data this does not mean that there cannot be routines of good practice. Good practice includes, keeping close to the data and maintaining the fit. Turner (1985) suggests engaging in comprehensive description of labels. Other advice, for example from Henwood and Pidgeon (1993, pp.23-27) includes keeping research memoranda; continually reflecting upon researchers' and analysts' values; keeping journals; building up documentation which includes much about the process of the research project, such as sampling decisions, hunches, and the context of data collection; testing out the generated theory with the participants, such that they should be able to recognise it; and finally, transferability.

In this study a number of these processes were engaged in. Initially there were research workshops where the team exchanged ideas and methods. Each researcher kept a notebook and there were frequent discussion sessions about the progress of the data collection, and changes made and recorded where necessary. Newspaper archives were studied to generate contextual material, and a launch workshop was used as a general discussion forum for the same purpose. Once initial analyses had been made of the data, tentative findings were fed back to a group of participants and others for their views on the representativeness and realism of the results so far.

There are some limitations to the method of collecting data used in this study. Perhaps the most important is that, by using a life history review through means of semi-structured interviews the participants were being asked to recall both their behaviour and emotions. They were not being observed as the events happened, nor were they keeping concurrent diaries over a number of years. The extent to which recall of past events is re-interpreted in the present must be questioned. However, the individuals who took part in the study did seem to be able to recall their behaviour and feelings at particular times, and differentiate these from how they would behave and feel at other times, when probed on how they would act now in similar circumstances.

The second limitation arises during analysis of the tape recorded material, when the extent to which the analyst selectively perceives what is heard on the tapes must be questioned. One way to minimise selectivity would be to use more than one analyst, and look for consistency between interpretations. In the case of the present study both reflected on similar emergent issues.

Data analysis technique

Obviously, without an organising framework, provided by an a prior theory, a substantial task confronting a researcher is to make use of considerable amounts of rich but unstructured data. This has implications for a number of aspects to the research, for example the indexing of material. On occasion the researcher has to have flexible terminological boundaries. She or he is not working to a set of pre-determined categories that would be mutually exclusive. One phenomenon might be tagged under a number of differing headings.

Involved in this process are creative and interpretative powers. Any descriptions applied must have an element of meaningfulness about them. Glaser and Strauss (1967), in their notion of grounded theory insist, as does Turner (1981) that such descriptions should fit the data well. Theories evolve as a result of reflection on and analysis of qualitative data, thus a tension is established between the researcher's own thoughts and the requirement of a justifiable fit.

The task before the researcher-analyst, is to build up from at first seemingly disparate categories coherent theoretical proposals. There are a range of associated techniques for this, many of which are listed by Henwood and Pidgeon (1993) as follows:

coding of instances until no new examples of variation are found; writing definitions of categories that are so derived; linking categories together, which will in turn provide new categories (p.21-22).

Consideration of coded and re-coded statements made by the interviewees resulted in the emergence of a number of clusters of factors reported here.

The analysis and analysts

This study is about women. It does not compare women to men, although data was also collected from men for the WIPL project. It is about a very particular aspect of some of a very few women's lives. It is about those women who work in managerial roles in a very specific type of organisation. It aims to contribute to the pool of accumulating information world wide that seeks to either understand or explain (or both) the nature of women's working lives, and this study is quite firmly placed in the realm of understanding, and not explaining.

Since this study is qualitative in nature and it is recommended that the 'knower should not be split off from the known, the first point of this analysis concerns the researchers. Who are they? All four are women, (although this is not true of the whole project). Two were Ghanaian research assistants, who generally interviewed the more junior women, closer in age, family and employment status to their own experience. Another researcher was a Nigerian scholar and writer (Dr Amina Mama)[3], with some experience of Ghana, who had also been concerned with management training for women from East Africa. The last, myself, is a British woman, an academic concerned with education management, and in particular such education for women and researching women in the public sector, which draws on my experience as a senior civil servant.

The particular commitment to the field of study and identification with it of the researchers, is particularly pertinent at the analysis phase, as in our engagement with the project we bring individual appraisals of the meanings and implications of the data we gathered. Our analyses reflect the standpoints we each take. Thus my analysis, reflecting my unique knowledge and experience, may differ from those of others surveying the material available, and is part of the context which, as recommended by Henwood and Pidgeon (1993) should be acknowledged in defence of a qualitative approach.

Results: emergent concepts and themes

As my analysis of the career life histories of the interviewees progressed, clusters of factors which interacted with individuals behaviour and career choices began to emerge. One cluster coalesces around the issues of work motivations, aspirations and expectations. This cluster largely focuses on processes within the individual. A second cluster could be summarised as to do with gender role socialisation, and is largely a function of dynamics between the individual and others. A third relates to opportunity and lack of it, that is largely contextual structures surrounding the individual which are outside her direct control. These structures of opportunity and dis-opportunity were also contained within a more distant set of general environmental factors such as culture, the socio-economic situation of the country and political matters.

These items may be grouped together and would seem to form a descriptive process (see figure 3.1). This suggests that the situation a woman ends up in her career is an interweaving of each of the clusters of items listed above. For each individual this will be unique, the model has no generally predictive capacity but it can help to explain what might be important, relevant, an aspect of process, and an aid to understanding, when designing policy, action and training to assist women to operate as they would wish in the workplace.

There are similarities between this proposed model and those presented by Astin (1984) and Hansen (1984). However, they tend to suggest there are causative linkages between similar sets of factors which they identify, whereas the author would not go so far as to claim causation. The clusters of factors and the linkages between them contribute to an understanding of career and work behaviour in each individual women, and such behaviour itself may feedback to the individual herself and the broader society.

Each of these factors interacts with women's career decisions and behaviour and women's career decisions and behaviour have the potential either to reinforce or to challenge the prejudices and stereotypes held about them, however unjust and discriminatory reactions based on these might be.

Essentially it is claimed that women's career choice and behaviour are related to personal motivations, aspirations and expectations about work, to the opportunity/dis-opportunity structures surrounding an individual, and the effects of sex-role socialisation. The structure of opportunity not only consists of the jobs available to women, but such things as family constraints, control over childbearing, personal characteristics and so on. Gender role socialisation takes place in the home, at school, during play and at work.

38

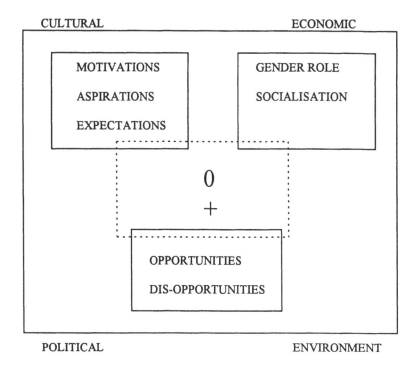

Figure 3.1 Clustered factors which interact with career development

Aspirations might consist of dreams which may not be achieved, or achievable, but which nonetheless are there despite sex role socialisation dynamics or lack of realistic opportunity, and probably feed into motivations. Expectations about what can be achieved at work, in a career, and are predicated on a barely conscious calculus concerning many of the factors that make up each of these clusters, including prior expectations.

Thus, the claim being made here is that each of these factors are important to the career development of women and their roles in management in the Civil Service of Ghana. Selected illustrations from the interviewees will be made, in order to support this judgement. Then how these insights can be used to inform policy, actions and, where appropriate, training shall be discussed.

Motivations, aspirations and expectations

These three concepts are related, and sometimes are interchanged in common usage, but they are separated here although comprising one cluster of factors internal to the individual.

Motivations relate not only to why people work, the simplest answer is for money, but why they choose the particular work they are engaged in, and why they display particular kinds of behaviour at work. Aspirations relate to what an individual dreams of doing, in the sense that Gould (1978) uses the term of a life dream. They also relate to the ultimate goal that an individual would hope to achieve, in this case in their career. Expectations concern what people think might happen to them, such as what grade they expect to be promoted to, not where they would wish to be promoted to, or what sort of interesting work they might realistically be given, not what they would like to get. Each of these factors which influence career development and job behaviour are discussed in turn and illustrations taken from the interview material.

Motivation

Not one of the civil servants interviewed mentioned that she had wanted to be a civil servant, in, for example, the same way a doctor or teacher might talk about her vocation.

Despite lack of individual conviction to be a civil servant, within Ghana there is general experience among the population that a public sector job is valuable, and worth entering. Such views are promoted by schools as well as individuals. Both a girl's school and her parents might well advise a job in the Civil Service, and the girl herself would not question this as a suitable career destination.

The reasons for the value placed on such employment include, secure employment, (until comparatively recently), and although not particularly well paid, access to housing, a degree of status, and the fact that the Civil Service will employ women as well as men. It is seen as less discriminatory on the grounds of gender than other employers such as the private sector might be.

There was a sense among the interviewees that they just fell into the civil service, that it was convenient. Most left education and went straight into the public sector. The alternatives available to such women would probably be teaching or medicine, and indeed a number of the interviewees did come into the service through teaching, although we deliberately did not sample the education ministry.

This acceptance of their profession is not to say that all were currently happy with their career choice. A number of interviewees indicated that they were looking elsewhere, towards the private sector or to NGOs. On the other hand it did not mean that individuals were not concerned to put their best efforts into the job, or that they were not motivated at that level. Most did seem to be highly motivated, for example, 'Sometimes I stay here until 10-11pm, I am asked if I have forgotten my husband'.

The need to advise younger colleagues to 'work hard' was commonly expressed. The potential of promotion seemed to be a major motivating dynamic amongst the interviewees. Many considered their rise to higher ranks a result of hard work. They frequently claimed they needed to work harder than men.

This is interesting because much of the general literature on this subject is ambivalent about the rewards for women of hard work. In addition women usually have the care of a household or family to attend to, to a far greater extent than men (see for example, Nicholson, 1996, Ch 5; Kanter, 1977, p.212-220; Collinson et. al., 1992). It does seem particularly unfair that a woman civil servant should expect herself to work hard (or harder) in the office and also carry out these home responsibilities. This would seem a sure way to burn-out, through stress.

In other studies (Wilson, 1991, Amos-Wilson, 1993) I have found that for women motivation is not only linked to extrinsic rewards such as pay and promotion but also to the opportunity to use education or to do something worthwhile. This was reflected here too, although quite commonly in a negative way. Individuals commented on being de-motivated because their education was not used. 'I do the technical work here but feel it is not recognised' 'I am not satisfied with my job because the work just trickles in and I think I am capable of doing more'.

Aspirations

It is not always possible to separate out career from more general aspirations. Aspirations play an important part in human development. One of the perspectives of this study is that of adult development. Theorists such as Havighurst (1972) and Gould (1972) position the role of aspirations, or dreams as a motivating force. The notion is that as young people we all develop a 'life script' a fantasy of what life should be like when we are older. We have role models around us which feed these dreams, and, if we are lucky, experiences and education which help us to shape these dreams. As adults we will re-evaluate these aspirations in the light of our experience and our opportunities, but some we may never lose sight of completely.

Theorists hold that it is the tension between aspirations and actuality which can give rise to discomfort at certain periods of life. Such discomforts can be perhaps triggered by the ageing process, or some life trauma, and occur particularly if we feel that we will never be able to fulfil our dreams to an adequate extent (Levinson, 1978). It is the drive to fulfil these aspirations that leads us to certain behaviour, including career behaviour.

Among commonly held aspirations are those connected with personal status and advancement, related in many cases to income. However there are also both culturally specific and gender factors which influence aspirations. Many women aspire to be 'good' mothers, and the interviewees were no exception to this.

For most respondents aspirations included both the desire to leave the civil service and concern about the extent to which reproductive work would interfere with other life aspirations. Those who planned to leave the service frequently talked about completely different forms of occupation, which may be voluntary rather than paid employment.

Very senior respondents were reticent about their employment related ambitions, but this could be a result of the fact that for the most senior, future advancement would be on a political basis.

With respect to their civil service career some of the participants were beginning to feel that this would not enable them to fulfil their aspirations sufficiently, and this was expressed in seeking alternatives, either in addition to the job, through, for example voluntary work, or in another occupation. Motherhood in general was not mentioned by many as the centre of women's aspirations. Frequently it seemed to be a necessary inconvenience to achievement of aspirations in the work career. The quotations below reflect a number of these issues.

I hope to do more in my church

I want to do something worthwhile, branching into the law or accounting. I hope to leave the Civil Service - no woman would join the civil service if you can get a better place.

Given the retrenchment of Civil Service jobs perhaps training for women should deal with the wider aspects of personal development and alternative employments of skills.

Of those that believed they were going to remain in the Civil Service and wanted to get on, many considered the only way to do so was to undertake private training courses.

The aspiration to be a 'good' mother can often seem at odds with that of hard worker, and a number of interviewees made this point, reflecting feelings of both guilt and role overload.

One statement seems to summarise personal conflicts that may arise within women concerning their aspirations.

Our role is not in the kitchen you need a determination to succeed. Marriage and kids are a barrier, one needs a sound mind.

Expectations

Expectations refer to the status, work, role, and rewards, including promotion that the interviewees expected to obtain. This is differentiated from what they aspired to obtain and what they felt might be their just desserts.

Many of the senior respondents had not expected to receive the promotions they had had, and in general junior women did not expect to receive appropriate rewards, including promotion, for their efforts.

A considerable number of the women felt they were unfairly discriminated against. More than once we were told 'Women can do anything a man can do'. There was a feeling present that women would not do as well as men, simply because of discrimination. Thus expectations were lowered, surprise being expressed when a woman got a justified position or reward. The majority reported some personal experience of gender discrimination which seemed related to expectations, but on the other hand they were encouraged and somewhat surprised when they received support from others, especially their supervisors.

In order to express feelings of unfair treatment, the individuals concerned must hold some notion of what they consider just, in other words have certain expectations, at the very least of equal treatment, and these expectations appear to have been depressed. This dynamic would seem problematic.

Gender role socialisation

If gender role socialisation with respect to paid employment did not exist in Ghana, it would be a matter of considerable surprise, and unique in the world. Thus the researchers on this project did expect to find gender role socialisation with respect to work among the women interviewed, and they were not disappointed. However, such socialisation, although it universally occurs, is also culture specific, and here culture is not necessarily taken to mean a whole nation, it may be specific as to a certain region, tribe, religion, generation and so on.

There was plenty of illustration that gender role socialisation did occur in the family, at school, in the workplace, and in society at large. All interviewees were asked about parental attitude to the education of girls, in comparison with boys in the family. Most of the interviewees reported very positive attitudes. Moreover the driving force behind this was frequently a mother who herself had received little or no education and who would work in order that her children should get a better opportunity in life. However the majority of fathers were also reported to have very positive attitudes towards their daughters' education.

For very many of the more senior women their fathers were much more highly educated than the general population even if their mothers were not. This seems to be reflective of comparatively recent changes in Ghanaian society with respect to education, overlaid by cultural attitudes, for example

> My father was highly educated and his attitude was that all his children must have sufficient education but my problem was that being a Moslem, by the time I had finished form five ... my grandmother was still alive and wanted me married, so that was a problem. I had to get married but at least I had my secondary education ... under normal circumstances I should have continued to the sixth form and maybe go to university, I tried but I had to stop because immediately after getting married I became pregnant with my first child.

In a few cases husbands had been instrumental in encouraging and supporting their wives through education they had missed out on earlier.

It seems also that the attitude of school was important too. Thus from the point of view of socialisation in connection with education and possibly through education it seems that boys and girls in the sample interviewed were treated equally, but of course socialisation also occurs in the home and the workplace.

Information was not specifically gathered from the interviewees about their experiences in their homes as children, in which case the participants would have been asked to recall events that happened some time ago. Instead it was sought through a discussion of how they arranged their own household affairs, what they expected husbands, children, members of the household and any staff to do. This could be seen as a proxy for how the individuals themselves had experienced socialisation in the home, the assumption being that they continued to transmit it in their own households to some extent. There were instances of gender differentiation being both present and not present.

For example many women did refer to their husbands 'helping' at home, and frequently described how chores were separated out, although these varied from family to family. The household structures therefore reflected notions of pre-egalitarianism (Berk, 1985; Mederer, 1993). Some of the interviewees required all their children, regardless of sex to help with all the chores in the house, whereas others had specific tasks for the boys, such as cleaning the yard, and for the girls, such as cooking.

Gender role socialisation at work probably very significantly affects this group of women, but this is not particularly easy to tease out from what is said.

When asked whether they believed being a woman had helped or hindered their career, most of the women were either ambivalent about this, or thought it positive. Paradoxically most were also able to recount instances where they had not been able to do something at work because of their gender, or indeed had suffered unpleasant situations, such as harassment, which can be viewed as an extreme attempt to socialise women into certain roles and behaviours at work.

A number of the interviewees reported that they had not been allowed to attend training courses, although it was their turn. Others reported being passed over for housing, one was told that 'houses are meant for men, not single women', or official cars.

A difficulty seemed to arise for some individuals in knowing what to do about an unfair situation predicated on the grounds of their sex. In particular a number of interviewees felt it was wrong for women to undertake what they termed lobbying.

> I wanted him to do something for me about the problem I had but he said you are a young woman and pretty so if I do it for you people will say that even if you deserved it it was just because I was a woman. I am sure that if it was a man who wanted to get on he wouldn't have minded lobbying and getting ahead, but being a woman stops me because you never know what people are going to say.

These statements could be seen as yet more examples of internalised gender role socialisation, of what is neither seemly, nor productive for a woman to undertake. There was a feeling that attempting to exert justified pressure would generate a negative backlash.

As is the case universally, there were very few women in the most senior roles and the reason why this is so are generally rehearsed. World wide women do not get organisational power equal to that of men but it is interesting to reflect on the specifics in the case of Ghana.

Ghana in common with other West African states has a tradition of women being in public, if not in the public sector, as traders. In fact many of the women interviewed owed their opportunity to access education to their mothers working as traders in order to be able to afford school fees. Ghana is also a matrilineal society, with the role of Queen Mother seen as important, and these are not only tribal roles, they are also the titles taken by important women traders. Yet even with this history of visibility and at least some economic power, women are still no more evident in senior positions than they are in other public sectors elsewhere.

Such a dynamic affects not only senior women but is evident throughout the organisation. The secretarial training college for the civil service trains only women, yet all but one of the senior posts in the College are held by men. Even in traditional public sector employments for women such as education, although there were a greater number of women in senior posts in this ministry than in any of the others, women still did not predominate at the top. Furthermore even senior women could be subjected to harassment.

Such harassment might be very direct physical assault, but frequently what was reported were actions of an unpleasant and nuisance type. Individuals were pestered for romantic relationships, or had their private lives publicly questioned or paraded, in ways that did not happen to men. In each case the intention, and very often the result, although not always at a conscious level, was to keep the woman concerned in her place.

Women suffered excessive enquiry into their private lives, the implications being that somehow a woman's role was to be virtuous, summed up by one respondent as;

They simply would not question a man about his private life in the same way.

The women themselves contributed, albeit unwittingly, to the socialisation process in the images of successful managerial women in the Civil Service. They were specifically asked their advice for someone entering the service who wanted to succeed. The replies were almost uniform.

Interviewees repeatedly told us that to achieve success a woman had to study hard at school and work hard in employment. Investment of effort in learning and working hard would eventually bring about the deferred gratification of a good job. Equally important was that women know how to conduct themselves, and here was meant in particular to conduct themselves properly with their male colleagues. They were to keep themselves aloof from any sexual advances, to maintain their reputation and not to give into male pressure. There was also the suggestion that women had to be particularly resilient,

if they (men) knock you down you just have to pick yourself up again.

Thus a woman who had reached a senior position would have been hard working, diligent, beyond reproach, resilient. These views seemed to indicate the feeling that somehow women are responsible for their own destiny, that as they probably will be victims of gender discrimination, they had better just get on with it, and do what they believed was required of them.

Although realising that such behaviours were demanded of them some of the interviewees did not feel they had suffered a particularly hard time achieving important status. They felt that if a girl applied herself as they had done she too

46

would eventually do well. For these women there was little acknowledgement of the role that structures of opportunity or dis-opportunity had played in the construction of their successful careers. However, this attitude was by no means the most commonly held. Many of the individuals concerned had travelled a difficult path to their position, and there was frequently the pressure of knowing that one false step now could destroy what had been achieved. They had to continue to be hard working, resilient and as one put it 'pure'.

Structures of opportunity and dis-opportunity

Structures of opportunity do not only include factors that could be seen as directly enabling or positive, for example, class, education, good quality work, promotion opportunities but also factors which enable individuals to take advantage of such opportunities or conversely those which disadvantage. One area where such enabling or disabling factors may abound is that of family relationships and care. In other words a woman's total position in her family, her role and non-work activities can impinge to a very great extent on the opportunities she is able to take up. For example in the Civil Service mobility is often a requirement, and frequently this is a condition that fewer women than men can comply with because of family responsibilities. If opportunity is predicated on mobility then women are bound to lose out.

Dis-opportunity in the form of supervisors damaging a woman's progress did seem to occur but it has to be said that this interference may or may not have been conscious. Thus, for example, a manager may have felt he or she could not give a particular task to a woman because it was assumed that the woman may have too many family responsibilities and should not be put under so much pressure. Frequently however, decisions of this type were made with no attempt to consult the woman concerned.

One of the most problematic areas of dis-opportunity is that of sexual harassment, and this was also reported by the interviewees.

A number of arenas in which opportunity and dis-opportunity occur can be identified. These are presented in figure 3.2 and each is considered in turn.

1.	Education and Training
2.	Family Situation
3.	Job
	roles
	gender distribution
	random assignments
	support in
4.	Support Structures
5.	Organisational structures and changes
6.	Harassment and Bullying

Figure 3.2 Arenas in which opportunities/dis-opportunities can occur

Education and training

Most of the interviewees in senior posts had very positive pre-work educational experiences in that they achieved the required diplomas and certificates which are entry requirements to the Civil Service. Thus in a mechanistic way the opportunities opened by education were available to them.

Once in post there was less evidence of planned careers, and training towards developing the individual, except for attendance at standard courses at the Ghanaian Institute of Management and Public Administration, where all Civil Servants undertake a variety of courses.

In fact in a number of cases individuals felt that they had been discriminated against with respect to formal training at work because they were women, or that they were not given jobs which would teach additional skills.

Interviewers asked if the individual's parents had had positive attitudes towards girl's education and this was overwhelmingly the case and the women concerned did in many cases attend 'top' schools and go onto higher education. Once in post some were enabled to follow post-graduate studies, frequently overseas. The subjects studied did tend to be predominantly humanities and social sciences. Science and mathematical subjects were less apparent. This is generally to be expected amongst both male and female civil servants.

The women themselves placed a very high premium on education and almost all recommended it as a path to later success for those that would follow them into the public service.

It was clear that the women had a number of expectations of the opportunities that a high level of education would bring them, which have not been fully realised. However, without these levels of education these individuals would not have proceeded even as far as they had. It may be said that it is certainly a necessary, if not sufficient condition.

Family situation

The overwhelming majority of the women were married, although not all were living with their spouses currently. Most had children, and some had live-in relatives. There is no doubt that all the women, married single or separated were involved in what can be termed family work. The manner in which they fulfilled their responsibilities under this heading varied. For example some undertook considerable childcare activities. These were not only contingent on number and age of children, but also of significance were whether the children were living at home, or away at school, whether other members of the immediate family, husband or siblings shared the care, or members of the extended family or paid help did so, and whether the children themselves 'helped' around the house.

Tasks most frequently reported by the interviewees as being undertaken by themselves in addition to family care included cooking and marketing. In general the overall image was of the woman being the person responsible for the management of the home and family, with other members 'helping' her. Such a management burden clearly could interfere with work responsibilities and opportunities to be had there. For example, in many organisations promotion is positively correlated with hours spent at work. The evidence from the interviewees would tend to support this. Women did report that they were expected to work late, and they did attribute negative discrimination with respect to promotion to their unwillingness to do this or the impossibility of compliance with this demand.

About jobs

We did not uncover any particular evidence in the civil service of career planning other than the administrative system of promotion on seniority. Almost all of the interviewees commented on the fact that their promotion had been slower than expected, but all also reported that this was because of a general freeze in Civil Service promotions during the late 1980s, which they were unlucky enough to suffer.

Occasionally women were put into particular jobs because of their perceived talents or developmental needs but this was not systematic.

Being placed in roles that are challenging, that give the individual the chance to develop and to achieve is an important aspect of the structure of opportunity. In order to progress an individual has to build personal capacity throughout their career and also be able to demonstrate to their managers their capabilities. If they are given only mediocre jobs below their capacity, as well as being de-motivating it will lead to dis-opportunity

Support structures

As aspects of support in the job, effective mentoring and adequate role models are related to opportunities. Many women reported that they felt there were few role models who had been available to them in their career, and conscious of this were trying to perform this role themselves for the next generation.

When specifically asked about individuals who may have influenced them a number could identify those who could be termed informal mentors, ranging from their own grandmothers to colleagues at work, including men. There appeared however no indication of formal mentoring systems within the workplace.

Role models and mentors are now seen as significant factors in encouraging individuals to think about what they are doing at work and to plan their opportunities. They are also part of the networks necessary to develop a career.

There was little evidence of support networks developing among the participants within the work context. The most senior women did try to support each other, but juniors reported understandable lack of interest, because of family time constraints etc. The women did however belong to numerous networks outside work, such as those associated with churches and these did seem to have some significance for the workplace.

Organisational factors

Nearly everyone involved in the study was affected by organisational changes, mostly disadvantageously. For many individuals, change resulted in a move to another ministry, or a delay in promised promotion. Sometimes a move expanded an individual's repertoire of skills, sometimes, especially where the individual was not mobile, it led to a loss of status, interesting work and general opportunity.

These did occur. Harassment whether sexual or forms of bullying is a means of preventing individuals' access to opportunities, through socialising them via violence to certain roles. It is not always conscious.

The environment in general

In many parts of the world today the public servant feels under threat. The drive is on to reduce the proportion of GDP that is spent on the public sector, and much of this reduction is achieved through increases in productivity which frequently involve savings in staff costs. Thus today the public servant in comparison with her or his predecessor may have to work harder, or longer, may have cuts in salary, or other benefits provided with the employment such as subsidised housing, healthcare schemes etc. and certainly does not feel that they have a secure job for life. Ghana is no exception to this world wide phenomenon.

Nonetheless the atmosphere of cut-back and retrenchment has done nothing to make Ghanaian women feel secure in their jobs, and almost everyone has to find additional means to stretch their seemingly inadequate incomes.

Unlike many other countries the political system in Ghana is currently stable and shows no sign of being otherwise. This does provide a sound basis for reforms in public administration, which are well underway and include an awareness of the need to employ all human resources effectively regardless of individuals non job related characteristics, such as gender.

Hence while on the one hand women may feel there are fewer opportunities available to them because of the current economic situation, socio-political forces are probably quite supportive of positive change.

Deeper level cultural mores concerning the role of women in the nation are, as elsewhere, present, but with respect to women in the public sector they do not necessarily have any particular Ghanaian gloss on them. (unlike for example Saudi Arabia where parallel male and female staffed ministries have been set up). Different cultures within the country do produce differing attitudes, for example we found a little evidence of difference between Muslim and non-Muslim attitudes towards women and family, but among the women we interviewed these were not significant. What is important is access to higher education, and many commented that their mothers had been very positively disposed towards this for their daughters. However such education generally steered individuals to enter the public service. We did not research attitudes towards women in the private sector, which can, of course range from the market traders to large multi-nationals, but perhaps there would not have been the emphasis on public sector employment for these women if other avenues had been available. It may be a case of the public sector not being particularly good but as a number commented, in one way or another, 'that was all there was'.

Themes from the Civil Service data and implications for policies, actions and training

The analysis above, suggests an interaction of a number of factors which influence the progress of any one individuals career. However from the four clusters a set of other themes emerges, surrounding the behaviour and self identification of women in managerial roles in the Ghanaian Civil Service. These have implications for policies, actions and training.

The first, which emerges primarily from a consideration of motivations aspirations and expectations, is that being a managerial Civil Servant is seen as not being a particularly good job. Bound up with this are the under-use of education and the lack of developmental training, the lack of mentoring, ad hoc job opportunities and disruptive organisational change.

The second concerns the expectations concerning the behaviour of women at work. These include the belief that women must work hard, that they must not engage in or display what are thought to be immoral sexual behaviours, although the women themselves have little control over what is defined as such, that they should not lobby, and that there are certain tasks that women are not fitted to perform. This is related to findings concerning gender role socialisation, and structures of opportunity and dis-opportunity.

The third concerns the tensions between career and family, in particular practical household arrangements, the attitudes of the women themselves, and a context in which there appears to be a belief that balancing career and family is a bigger problem than it actually is. This relates to structures of opportunity and dis-opportunity.

The fourth concerns sexual harassment in the workplace, which relates to gender role socialisation, and dis-opportunity.

I will comment on each of these and put forward suggestions for policy, action and, where appropriate, training.

The perception that the Civil Service is not a good job

It is interesting that so many of the respondents were so de-motivated in the Civil Service that they were considering and hoping for employment elsewhere.

This may in part be due to low pay rates, but this is an issue that bears more investigation.

Even with better pay, I suspect that women would still wish to leave because the work is not seen as intrinsically interesting and rewarding. To some extent this is linked to the issue of little use being made of education and skills. What is suggested by this problem is the need to review the structuring and content of Civil Service managerial work, job evaluation and staff development. This is a sound personnel policy and is effective irrespective of gender considerations. An evaluation programme concentrates on the work to be done, not the individual doing it. The recommendations for policy and action here are a commitment to a review of the organisation and content of work within the civil service, and the actions necessary would include the implementation of organisational audits and job evaluation schemes. Training in these processes might be required for selected staff.

The under-use of education and the lack of developmental training contribute to de-motivation, but furthermore they are symptomatic of a lack of detailed knowledge about the individuals employed in the Civil Service. If one side of an effective deployment policy is an analysis of the job to be done, the other is an understanding of the human skills within an organisation. The implication for policy here is also commitment to a review of the human resource within the service and matching it to the range of tasks to be performed, and the actions and training implications are as above, an organisational audit, and training of personnel to conduct this. In addition a human resource development programme to enable those currently employed to express and develop skills to match what is required would be useful. Alongside this it would be advantageous to introduce an appraisal system that would ensure a continuing process of evaluation of staff development needs. This could also involve an effective mentoring system.

The implementation of an effective human resource deployment system would minimise the frequency of ad-hoc job placements and would also be a mechanism through which necessary organisational change would be mediated. In the majority of organisational change programmes reviews of jobs and personnel are necessary, and a system already in place and known to employees would be advantageous in these conditions.

Expectations concerning the behaviour of women at work

Such expectations are held by everyone in the workplace. Iᵣ many organisations it is often more comfortable for those about whom expectations are held to conform with these expectations. It is a brave woman who flouts convention for she will probably have to suffer personal criticism and sanctions against her (Kanter, 1977; Nicholson, 1996). In some cases just being there is sufficient violation of a convention for a woman to be treated badly. This is often the case for the first woman to be appointed to a particular role, such as the first head of a Civil Service Department, and we certainly found evidence of this.

What is also interesting about this theme as it emerges in this study is the views that the women themselves hold about appropriate behaviour, despite, or perhaps because of, having suffered a range of discriminatory behaviour and sanctions in many cases.

The first is the belief that hard work will result in just reward. This is despite evidence which the interviewees must have experienced to the contrary. It may well be the case that women who have achieved status have worked hard, but there is not necessarily a causal relationship. There may be many instances of women who have worked hard who have not achieved status, and men who have not worked hard who have achieved status. Moreover it is possible that senior women who hold this view may be tempted to do a disservice to junior women colleagues. There is scant evidence in the management literature that hard work is positively correlated with promotion, although there is some that working long hours is. There is plenty of evidence that gender is correlated with promotion. However, if women themselves assume it has been their hard work which has resulted in a senior position, they might believe that those women who have not achieved this are not hard workers, and not deserving of support (Kanter, 1977; Marshall, 1984; The Hansard Society, 1990; Jackson and Hirsch, 1991; Nicholson 1996).

The expectations of sexual propriety, which also involve a reluctance to lobby and the belief that there are certain job tasks, because of their nature, women are not fitted to perform are to be found among men and women in the Civil Service. Here I wish to discuss not these expectations themselves, but the unjust and unjustified assumptions that might surround them, some of which were illustrated in preceding sections.

As in many other societies, assumptions of sexual availability may be made about a woman who is not married, and she will both be prey to some male colleagues and also be seen as not respectable. One notable case of the public pillorying of a divorced government minister illustrates this. The individual concerned was subjected to the most public examination of her private life on the floor of the House of Parliament when she was proposed for a ministerial post. 'Unrespectable' women may be seen as not worthy of senior posts.

Even if a woman is married, but if she is attractive or friendly or helpful, or even just working in a male environment she too may be seen as sexually available, or not quite respectable. Furthermore a woman who engages in a relationship with a colleague may also be seen to be immoral and, if the man is in a senior position, using him to advance her career. Women are under very considerable pressure if they want to be seen as credible in their career to behave in a very constrained way and if they once let their guard slip their careers may be blighted for ever.

It is the assumptions that result in discriminatory and unjust decisions regarding women that require attention, and are particularly difficult to deal with.

The policy should be not to let such assumptions interfere with sound personnel decisions. Individuals should be assessed on their actual capacity or potential to undertake tasks. Methods of challenging assumptions need to be adopted, and these may include formal training and less formal discussion groups. In addition women themselves have a role to play through networking, personal conscientisation and generating support systems for each other. Such networks and systems may be women only but the inclusion of all those who are interested in objective organisational human resource assessment and the removal of inappropriate stereotyping and invalid attributions should be encouraged.

Tensions between career and family

The interesting feature about this theme is not that tension between career and family do exist for many women, but that these are very often perceived to be more important than they are by others than by the women involved. Generally speaking women evolve systems to cope with the practical difficulties. However assumptions often seem to be made by their managers that under certain circumstances the individual woman would not be able to comply with the demands of a job because of her domestic circumstances. Although this may occasionally be true, it is sometimes exaggerated in that more demanding work conditions are applied to women than to men, increasing the likelihood of their failure to meet the situation.

Much of the tension that exists for a woman is not that which would materially affect the performance of her job. Rather it is concerned with the mental and emotional tension she feels about the possibility of not being a 'good' mother, or indeed wife if she spends much of her day outside the home. It can be worse still if she enjoys her job. The word guilty is often used by women to represent these emotions.

The policy implications for the tension between family and career are related both to organisations and the individual. Organisations should be committed to ensuring that they enable all employees to perform effectively. In terms of action this may mean organising working practices to take account of the fact that most employees are family members too. Unsocial working hours affect men and women alike and may drive down performance. Working practises should be reviewed to consider both their task effectiveness and effective human resource deployment.

Individuals may need to reassess whether the feelings they have concerning their capacities as a parent or spouse are valid. Support networks can be useful here.

Sexual harassment in the workplace

This can be a serious detriment to the career development of women. As well as the direct aspect of the refusal to promote an individual because she will not provide sexual favours to her boss it also frequently lowers the self-esteem of the individual, affects her work performance, can have marked effects on her health generating extensive sick leave. None of these will contribute positively to her career development.

Sexual harassment is problematic not only because it occurs but also because frequently it is not clearly identified. A range of behaviours may be included in its definition and these will vary at the cultural as well as the individual level. One clear aspect of it however is that it is often about power, not sex, and is used by some men to control some women.

Organisations can do much to minimise sexual harassment in the workplace by instituting policies which outlaw the practice and discipline it perpetrators. However it is probably necessary because of the difficulties in definition to involve as many personnel as possible in the formulation of such policy. Both formal training and discussion groups have a role to play here.

Action needs to be taken both to inform all staff of the issues, procedures and penalties and to ensure that the policy is followed up if there are any breaches.

Concluding remarks

This chapter has examined aspects of women's career progression to senior managerial posts in the Ghanaian Civil Service. It has sought not to look at the more obvious processes of discrimination against women at work but has concentrated on listening to the voices of women themselves and drawing out themes. It was found that the data could be clustered into four broad areas, concerned with motivations, aspirations and expectations about work; with gender role socialisation; with structures of opportunity and dis-opportunity and with the general environmental context. From these areas four dominant themes emerged, within which individuals acted out work role behaviours and created managerial identities. These concern perceptions of the civil service as an employer; expectations about women's behaviour at work; the tension between career and family and finally sexual harassment. Suggestions for meeting these issues were put forward.

As I conclude, I should like to state that the findings obtained here, through the support of the Ghanaian women who took part are similar to those reported elsewhere by myself and others. Those women who took part in the study have contributed to an understanding of the dynamics of women at work and what informs and constrains the development of a managerial career for women. The implications discussed in the previous sections are relevant to many cultures and contexts.

The generosity of the participants in sharing aspects of their lives is much appreciated by me and I hope it will also be by those that read this chapter. I also hope that readers will feel that they can identify with the issues recounted and find some of the policy and action recommendations put forward useful.

Notes

1. This study was part of the Women in Public Life Project sponsored by the Government of Ghana and funded by the United Kingdom Department for International Development in Ghana. It was conducted by four institutions, The Institute of Statistical, Social and Economic Research at the University of Ghana; the Government Institute of Management and Public Administration, Ghana; The National Council for Women and Development, Ghana; and the Development and Project Planning Centre, University of Bradford, UK.

2. The Department of International Development (DFID) is the British Government Department which supports programmes and projects to promote international development. It provides funding for economic and social research to inform development policy and practice. DFID funds supported this pilot study and the preparation of the summary of findings. DFID distributes the report to bring the research to the attention of policy makers and practitioners. However, the views and opinions expressed in the documents do not reflect DFID's official policies or practices, but are those of the author alone.

3. Dr Amina Mama, of Nigeria an independent scholar and activist, also visiting lecturer to Bradford University; Christabel Mills and Hilda Aikin, post-graduate students of the School of Communications University of Ghana, and the author.

References

Amos-Wilson P M (1993), 'Accomplishing Career Development Tasks: are there gender related differences?' *International Journal of Career Development,* 5(5) pp.11-17.

Astin H S, (1984), 'The meaning of work in women's lives: A socio-psychological model of career choice and work behaviour', *The Counselling Psychologist,* 12(4), pp.117-126.

Berk, S, (1985), *The Gender Factory: The apportionment of Work in American Households,* New York, Plenum.

Bulmer M, (1979), 'Concepts in the Analysis of Qualitative Data', in Bulmer M (ed.) *Sociological Research Methods,* London, Macmillan.

Cicourel A V, (1964), *Method and Measurement in Sociology,* New York, Free Press.

Collinson D L, Knights D and Collinson M (1990), *Managing to Discriminate,* London, Routledge.

Denzin N K and Lincoln Y S, (1994), *Handbook of Qualitative Research,* London, Sage.

Dilthey W, (1977), 'Descriptive Psychology and Historical Understanding' (RM Zaner and K L Heiges, trans.) *The Hague, Martinus Nijhoff.* (original work published 1894).

Droyson J G, (1858), 'Gruindiss der Historick', cited in GH Von Wright, 'Two Traditions', in Hammersley, M *Social Research, Philosophy, Politics and Practice,* London, Sage.

Geertz C, (1973), *The Interpretation of Cultures,* New York, Basic Books.

Gellejeh S (1990), *A Study of Women in Management in Tanzania,* Institute of Management Development, Mzumbe.

Glaser B G and Strauss A L, (1967*), The Discovery of Grounded Theory: Strategies for Qualitative Research,* New York, Aldine.

Gould R L (1978), *Transformations: Growth and change in adult life,* New York, Simon and Schuster.

Gould T L (1972), 'The phases of adult life: A study in developmental psychology'. *American Journal of Psychiatry,* 129, pp.521-531.

Griffin C (1986), 'Its different for Girls: the use of qualitative methods in a study of young women's lives', in H Beloff (ed.), *Getting into Life,* London, Methuen.

Hammersley M, (1996), 'The relationship between qualitative and quantitative research: paradigm loyalty versus methodological eclecticism', in J T E Richardson (ed.) *Handbook of Qualitative Research Methods,* Derby, British Psychological Society.

The Hansard Society Commission, (1990), *Women at the Top*, London The Hansard Society.

Hansen J-I, (1984), 'Response to the meaning of work in women's lives', *The Counselling Psychologist*, 12(4) pp.147-149.

Harding S (1986), *The Science Question in Feminism*, Milton Keynes, Open University Press.

Harding S (1987), *Feminism and Methodology*, Milton Keynes, Open University Press.

Harding S (1991), *Whose Science? Whose Knowledge? Thinking from Women's lives*. Milton Keynes, Open University Press.

Harlley E (1995), Women in Public Service in Ghana, address to the launch of the Women in Public Life Project, Ghana, Accra, January 25.

Havighurst R J (1972), *Developmental Tasks and Education* (3rd edition) New York, David McKay.

Henwood and Pidgeon (1993), *Qualitative research and Psychological Theorizing, in Social Research: Philosophy, Politics and Practice*, M Hammersley (ed.), London, Sage.

Jackson C and Hirsch W (1989), Women in Management: Issues influencing the entry of women into managerial jobs, paper 158, Institute of Manpower Studies, Sussex University.

Jemerigbe H I (1992), Constraints to Women's Employment and Advancement to Top Management Position in Africa, conference paper Women in Top Management, African Association of Public Administration and Management, Banjul, Gambia, February 3-6.

Kanter R M (1977), *Men and Women of the Corporation*, New York, Basic Books.

Khan S (1992), *The fifty per-cent, Dhaka Bangladesh*, Dhaka Publishers.

Levinson D J, (1978), *The Seasons of a man's life*, New York, Ballantine.

Marshall J, (1984), *Women Managers: Travellers in a Male World*. Chichester, John Wiley.

Mederer H J, (1993), 'Division of Labour in two-earner homes: task accomplishment versus household management as critical variables in perceptions about family work' *Journal of Marriage and the Family*, vol 55, pp.133-45.

Nicholson P, (1996), *Gender Power and Organisation: A Psychological Perspective*, London, Routledge.

Silverman D, (1993), *Interpreting Qualitative Data, Methods for analysing talk, text and interaction*, London, Sage.

Stanley L and Wise S (1983), *Breaking Out: Feminist Consciousness and Feminist Research*, London, Routledge and Kegan Paul.

Turner B A (1981), 'Some practical aspects of qualitative data analysis: one way of organising some of the cognitive processes associated with the generation of grounded theory', *Quantity and Quality*, 15, pp.225-47.

Turner T and O' Connor P, (1994), 'Women in the Zambian Civil Service: a case of equal opportunities?' *Public Administration and Development* 14, pp.79-92.

Wetherall and Potter (1988), 'Discourse Analysis and the identification of interpretative memoirs' in C Antaki, (ed.), *Analysing everyday Explanation: A Casebook of Methods*, London, Sage.

Wilson P M (1991), 'Women Employees and Senior Management', *Personnel Review* 20(1).

Woolgar S (1996), 'Psychology, qualitative methods and the ideas of science', in J T E Richardson (ed.) *Handbook of Qualitative Research*, Derby, British Psychological Society.

4 HRM issues and implications of the process of 'localisation'

Harry Wes

Introduction

In this chapter attention is drawn to some of the issues of developing host country nationals, 'locals', to replace expatriate staff. Although training and development techniques will not be discussed the implications which they have will have to be considered by organisations and individuals when locals are taking over jobs from foreigners.

It is true that many of the issues that confront international Human Resource Management (HRM) specialists are similar to those concerning their domestic equivalent i.e. selection and retention of good performers, maximising their performance, maintaining staff motivation and doing all this in a cost effective way. However the ways of handling these issues may be different. Some of these differences will be outlined and several additional issues not faced by our domestic colleagues will be introduced.

Globalisation

Globalisation is seen by many organisations as the key to competitive advantage in production and marketing (Bartlett, 1990). Whilst it is undoubtedly true that international cross flows of materials and products will be crucial to the development of a healthy world economy and a general raising of standards of living the complex organisational and human aspects of globalisation are often neglected.

Gone are the 'good old days' when anything that could be produced by the industrialised West could be sold. The customer could have anything he or she wanted so long as it was what the industrialist wanted to produce, and the expatriate could be sure of a well paid job telling foreigners what to do (Starkey, 1994; Mean, 1995).

Most transitional and developing countries are not impressed by the old conservative ways of the West and want their own citizens to hold important crucial decision making and senior jobs (Bedi, 1991). They do recognise that there are rarely sufficient Host Country Nationals (HCNs) with the competencies and experience to quickly take over from the expatriates. Expatriates will continue to be employed to do jobs for which there are insufficient HCNs willing or able to undertake. They do, however, want to be sure that organisations operating in their countries are willing to see their nationals as competent skilled workers and managers not merely docile producers or consumers of whatever the Western organisation chooses to make and sell.

Growing confidence of governments in transitional and developing countries causes them to be more strict with legislation and rules regarding employment of expatriates- especially in connection with qualifications. A white skin is no longer an automatic ticket for a work permit!

Innovation and conservatism

Western management and workers are very conservative in comparison to those of the East. Western companies prefer steady expansion and fear overextending and so falling into the hands of receivers or competitors. It is common, however, in the rapidly expanding economies of transitional and developing countries, for plans to underestimate the expansion of markets and facilities rather than to be over optimistic in their expectations.

Western managers think that they know all the answers and that every where else is developing to catch up (Hailey, 1994). Most human beings are resistant to changes in their circumstances, especially if the change is likely to be adverse in terms of income, career prospects and job security. In many organisations seeking to become 'global', all the senior management posts are likely to be held by parent country nationals or Caucasian expatriates (Banai, 1992). They are often resistant to the development of local nationals to fill positions of power.

Selection

Many organisations of the developing world employing expatriates do not select in the sophisticated way generally used in large organisations in the

Western world. Often this is due to the paternalistic management style favoured in the developing world. Amongst the factors which might cause this are reliance upon family firms and public organisations, the size of the organisation, the maturity or organisational development since inception, the geographic location and the culture of the society in which the organisation is based (Warner, 1993). There is a need to pay attention to the work of Hofstede (1980), and Trompenaars (1993) on cultural factors differentiating societies and organisations. Although there has been some criticism of their research (d'Iribarne, 1989). The author believes that they have made a valuable contribution to international organisational development.

Expatriates may try to be objective in selection but more often than not will be influenced in selection by language skills of nationals and third country nationals. They will tend (as many HR people and other managers tend to do) to try to select people like themselves or others they consider to be 'good' employees. This will encourage ethnocentricity especially in so called multinational organisations. To host country managers the family background, political connection and racial group of candidates for appointment or promotion can be more important than ability (Bedi, 1991). Some might argue that the Western view of discrimination on the grounds of ability is unethical as the weak members of society who lack ability are not protected e.g. rural Bumiputras in Malaysia (Mahathir, 1981). These factors and facts are difficult for Western trained managers to cope with, hence the ability to handle ambiguity regularly emphasised by effective HR practitioners.

Even when apparently sophisticated techniques are used i.e. psychometric tests or competencies it is rare for those to be normed or adapted for the region in which the organisation operates (Welch, 1994). For example clerical ability tests are often developed in the West to analyse skills of those with basic secondary or High school education but in some places, such as South Asia, clerical jobs are carried out by low paid but graduate level employees. The techniques used need to be adapted to the local environment.

Performance management

Much of the theory of Performance management is grounded in societies which are predominantly Anglo-Saxon Protestant and Capitalist, especially the United States of America. In the USA there is general acceptance of frank speaking between supervisor and subordinate (Hofstede, 1980; Trompenaars, 1993). It is expected that people are told about their shortcomings and that they be rewarded (or compensated!) for good performance. In the mobile employment market, in which most employees do not even have a contract of employment, poor performers quickly find themselves without a job and good performers who are not well paid or well treated will soon find another job. It is important that the employer and employee understand the perceptions and expectations of the other. In the USA, and increasingly in Europe, the risk of law suits for negligence or discrimination probably add an extra incentive to develop formal performance reviews which may not fit into some societies in Africa, Asia or South America.

In much of the world outside the USA it is less easy for supervisors and subordinates to be open about their views. This may be due to expectations about the seniority in terms of age or status of those involved, to issues of 'face', which do not only arise in the East, or to the involvement of Trade Unions who do not want individuals to be treated in ways that do not apply to others in a group (Warner, 1993). It is very difficult to persuade supervisors in many parts of the world to be honest with subordinates about their short falls or to make recommendations about pay that do not reflect the subordinates personal circumstances rather than their work performance e.g. the wedding of a daughter or education of a son. It is often inconceivable to reward a younger or junior employee at a higher rate than an older/more senior employee because issues beyond those of immediate pay or promotion are involved.

It is common for domestic companies in much of the world to not publish reliable financial accounts so it is difficult for both supervisors and subordinates to be certain of their contribution to the organisation's performance. In the case of Multinational or International companies transfer pricing can have the same effect of obscuring the true profitability of the local organisation.

This is not to say that the International Human Resource Manager should not try to improve the performance of the workforce but there may be a need for more subtlety than in the USA. There may be a need to set 'softer' or more easily attainable targets initially so that staff become familiar and at ease with the concept of performance management as well as discussion about ability and achievement (Hofstede, 1980).

Remuneration

The way in which we rewarded staff for their efforts becomes more complex. Expatriates have to be paid enough to stop them going to employers who might offer longer term employment prospects (Welch, 1994) - at least before a Host Country National is trained and ready to take over. On the other hand the company can not pay nationals who replace the expatriates the full range of salary and benefits which had been necessary to hold the previous postholders on a short term contract.

The company might fix a salary for the job but also add on inducements such as education allowances, end of service bonus payments and other items (Mendenhall, 1987). These do not fit in well with the type of 'clean wage' policy which most Western HRM practitioners prefer. 'Clean wage' policies appear to be transparent and consistent - even if it is not always so in practice.

A particular factor that does have to be considered with regard to payment for performance in expatriate situations, is that when employment is stable employees are prepared to make a concerted effort in expectation of a deferred reward. If, however, there is uncertainty of tenure a deferred reward is discounted. Staff wish to have the reward paid soon after the performance is achieved so will favour short term goals.

Host country nationals are also less likely to accept deferred reward and promises of future promotion into a job currently held by an expatriate if other employers are offering opportunities now.

Factors of status which are rarely issues in Europe and North America are sources of resentment in the expatriate/local environment. Those visible status symbols such as car and club membership cause particular resentment (Bedi, 1991). The host country nationals are reminded of perceived 'inferior status' each time they see the expatriate drive past in a company provided car on the way to the company paid for foreigner's club. When he replaces the expatriate it is not acceptable to be told that these facilities are only given to those temporarily in the country and will not be given to the local resident!

Unfortunately there is still too often a feeling that foreigners are paid too much and conversely that nationals are paid more than is justified by their performance at work. Even the use of comprehensive salary and benefits surveys such as those produced by Hay or ECA does not convince staff that their particular package is adequate for the work that they perform!

Motivation

The rapid growth and occasional rapid decline in economic fortunes of many organisations in transitional and developing societies has gradually led to expatriate and, to a lesser extent host country nationals, to move towards portfolio career patterns. These career patterns are likely to be common in developed societies in the future (Handy, 1995). No longer can a person joining an international organisation or a host country enterprise expect to be able to complete their career in the same organisation. This combined with the factors referred to under performance management will encourage expatriates to be risk adverse and will aim for short term rewards rather than long term career enhancing achievements (Brewster, 1991).

The expatriates who could be losing their privileged positions, if not their job, have to be persuaded to encourage those local citizens who might replace them. Host Country Nationals who fail to get to the front of the training or promotion queue know that in all probability they will spend the rest of their career in the shadow of those who had initially been only slightly ahead of them - waiting for promotion into 'dead men's shoes'. Maybe this situation will persist over a period of decades.

The expatriates who would eventually be replaced should be given opportunities, at the company's expense, to increase their portfolio of skills and qualification, so adding to their value to future employers. In too many cases the expatriates have been neglected and gradually their attractiveness to other employers is so low that they do not expect to get another reasonable job. Therefore, they do all they can to stay in their existing job and hold back the local national.

Expatriates will be discouraged when their remuneration fails to keep up with that of their home country contemporaries due to differences in relative rates of inflation or exchange rate fluctuations. To deal with this effect on morale, complicated exchange rate protection programmes have to be devised to cope with these problems which are not of the organisation's making. Such efforts intended to maintain expatriate morale can have an adverse effect on host country national's morale. The latter may already be upset at having to wait to take over from an expatriate when they consider that they already have the necessary capability.

Host country nationals may find themselves doing 'non-jobs', especially in government or quasi-government organisations or in public relations or liaison jobs in commercial companies (Muna, 1980). These non-jobs not only inflate payrolls, act as a tax on business and slowdown customer service but they also discourage others to perform or develop. Alternatively a national may be rushed into replacing an expatriate before he is trained and prepared and so fail to perform. Then many, locals as well as expatriates, can say 'I told you so' and the process of replacing expatriates is put back by a few more years (Potter, 1989).

In some cases because the host country nationals are promoted on the basis of time served, those fellow nationals who have devoted time to study and improved qualifications will find themselves beneath a less capable national not only at the beginning of a career but potentially for the majority of a career. If a host country national is appointed to replace an expatriate when he (it is invariably he) is in his late twenties/early thirties he forms a block on the appointment of others for maybe thirty years. That is indeed frustrating for those he beat to the job.

Training although mainly directed at host country nationals can be a useful motivator of expatriates by giving them abilities to add to their portfolio of skills which will help them to find a job later in their career.

Succession planning and other human resource plans

It is initially expensive to develop and implement an HR plan as a lot of management time goes into its production and extra resources are required for example to recruit and train unskilled staff instead of buying in trained foreigners. The investment in them is, however, of benefit to the organisation and the country for a long period.

A plan I drew up 16 years ago involved a series of manpower projections being constructed for each of the following 20 years (Harry, 1996). The requirements for the next year were known from the manpower budget, those of the next 3 years could be predicted from the operating plan but beyond that 'guestimates' had to be made. It is interesting that the HRM staff had to look way beyond the horizons established by the finance, commercial and operating departments.

HR planning is successful if the organisation achieves its business objectives including growth and profit as well as providing a quality service to customers at a price they are willing to pay. At the same time it must offer a chance to individuals to develop or maintain a satisfactory portfolio of skills and abilities which will be of value to them in their career in that organisation or another.

Costs

Often localisation is perceived as a cost saving exercise but in fact in the short term it is expensive (Kobrin, 1988). Usually there are more trained and experienced expatriates in the market than trained and experience host country nationals. Therefore those local people will attempt to sell their skills for at least as much as the expatriate.

In the past companies 'bought in' expatriates who had most of their expensive training paid for by former employers. The change to developing their own employees is expensive in the short term but more than pays for itself through having a workforce inculcated with 'our' culture and the loyalty from people who see that their employer is prepared to invest in their future.

Training budgets have to be increased by a substantial amount to pay for external training, in-house training and the appointment of supernumerary staff. These supernumerary staff may be nationals who are gaining work experience after training or foreigners who are assisting the newly appointed individuals until they are fully capable of performing the work of those they are replacing.

Conclusions

During my 16 or so years, as a manager, dealing with the issue of 'localisation' I generally held the view that it was the right of host country nationals to replace expatriates because 'it is their country'. I was concerned only with process by which this could be done most efficiently. Often in the quest for efficiency I and others lose effectiveness. Needless expatriate resistance and host national resentment is generated. The whole process of localisation is less effective than it could or should be.

References

Banai Moshe (1992), 'The Ethnocentric staffing policy in multinational corporations: a self-fulfilling prophecy', *International Journal of Human Resource Management*, vol. 3. 3 pp.451-472.

Bartlett C , Y Doz and G Hedlund (eds) (1990), *Building and Managing the Global Firm* London, Routledge.

Bedi Hari (1991), *Understanding the Asian Manager*, London, Allen and Unwin.

Brewster Chris (1991), *The Management of Expatriates*, London Kogan Page.

d'Iribarne Philipe (1989), *La Logique de l'honneur. Gestion des Entreprises et traditions Nationales*, Paris, Seuil.

Hailey John (1994), *'The Expatriate Myth'*, paper given at the EIASM Workshop on Cross Cultural Perspectives on Comparative Management and Organisation.

Handy Charles (1995), *Beyond Certainty,* London, Arrow Books.

Harry Wes (1996), 'High Flying Locals', *People Management,* pp.37 11 July.

Hofstede Geert (1980), *Culture's Consequences,* Beverley Hills, California Sage.

Kobrin Stephen J (1988), 'Expatriate reduction and strategic control in American Multinational Corporations' *Human Resource Management,* Spring, vol 27, number 1.

Mahathir Mohamad (1981), *The Malay Dilemma,* Kuala Lumpur, Malaysia Federal Publications.

Mead Richard (1995), *International Management: cross cultural dimensions,* Oxford, Blackwell.

Mendenhall M, E Dunbar and G Oddou (1987), 'Expatriate Selection, Training and Career Pathing', *Human Resource Management,* 26 (3) pp.331-345.

Muna Farid (1980), *The Arab Executive,* London, St. Martin's Press.

Potter Christopher C (1989), 'Effective localisation of the workforce', *Journal of European Industrial Training,* vol 14 no. 6 pp.25-30.

Starkey K and McKinlay A (1994), 'Managing for Ford', *Sociology,* vol 28 no 4. November pp.975-990.

Trompenaars Fons (1993), *Riding the Waves of Culture,* London Economist, Books.

Warner Malcolm (1993), 'Human Resource Management with Chinese Characteristics', *International Journal of Human Resource Management,* 4 (1) pp.45-62.

Welch Denise (1994), 'Determinates of International Human Resource Management Approaches and Activities', *Journal of Management Studies,* 31 (2) pp.149-174.

5 Tacit knowledge and HRD for development work

Pete Mann

Introduction

Tacit knowledge has to do with the learning we take for granted. It is hard to put into words. Later in the chapter I will contrast it with explicit or articulated knowledge, which relies upon words and systems for codifying and transmitting knowledge. Development work is the productive activity that people accomplish in changing their worlds and thereby themselves. Some in human resource development (HRD) believe for people to act on their environments they must first change themselves, that is, do the learning before the doing. I'm not sure how true this is. Perhaps it is for certain kinds of work and activity, like routine tasks (even complicated routines). Or in certain kinds of environments, where there is much empirical research to inform the way ahead. But development work is often not set in these circumstances. It deals with change, with making improvement or with strengthening human performance, often in contexts which themselves are changing (or perhaps haven't changed in decades), where human performance is already overstretched (or historically under-utilised). Development work often is breaking new ground - or so it can feel to some doing it. No precedents seems to apply, others' experience does not feel relevant. This 'particularistic feel' to development work sets it apart to them: nothing at the time is comparable, lessons elsewhere meaningless. For others, the aura of innovativeness or uncertainty in development work and the sense of being at the cutting edge are no big thing. For them, the improvement, the change, the challenge are simply business as usual. They are not caught up in the throes of practising it.

Development work becomes developmental in another way, too, for its practitioners. For these managers (or technically qualified people, or operatives, or professionals) it can lead to significant learning. In changing their worlds and themselves, people can learn the relationship between what 'is out there' and what 'can be in here', between reality and potency. In the jargon of HRD what they can learn is power relations. They learn directly the nature of ambiguity in coalitions of vested interests as they learn firsthand how to nurture decisiveness and collective will. In encountering the status quo they learn what dominance means by feeling both powerful and vulnerable as they engender their own and others' capacity. At times they probably learn much about the nature of power by experiencing their own effectiveness.

Good HRD enables people to learn along this continuum. But in itself 'good' HRD is a double-edged instrument: releasing, through ensuring that development work empowers, yet regulating by its systematic entry and exit, things like access and certification. The nature of this tension in the duality of HRD - liberating while constraining - can be de-constructed by a perspective on learning that questions the nature of knowledge for practising development work. The debates here will lead easily to further questioning of the nature of knowledge that is emphasised in postgraduate HRD provision for in-service or mid-career practitioners, like in accredited Masters programmes of management and organisational studies. One argument put forward is that there is something demanded in development work that is not sufficiently taken account of in the way human resources are prepared to practise it. This something is about conversion of knowledge between thought worlds, between the world of work and the world of thinking about work, between the world of know-how and the world of know-about, between the phenomenal and physical world and the phenomenological and metaphysical world. As a clash between world views, this knowledge conversion becomes problematic, like contestation between paradigms, where the dominance of the orthodox thought world rules supreme, demolishing non articulated knowledge of development practice like a champion pulverising a sparring partner. I wonder, in short, whether sufficient attention in the promotion of HRD for development work is given to the thought world in this chapter called tacit knowing.

The presentation of the chapter proceeds in congruence with the content of the argument. Dictates of reliance on explicit knowledge - the conventional knowledge through which we articulate discourse, for example - would necessitate the writer first define his terms. Indeed, two colleagues, both professors, kindly reviewed an early draft, and each independently proposed a change of format for the chapter. 'Start with ... tacit-explicit links', the first offered, as did the second: '... more clearly specify tacit knowledge in the introduction'. Academics are used to a syllabus and conspectus. Perhaps they assume a social order in which people are first taught, then go out into the world to make use of their acquired knowledge in leading productive lives. Some academics, steeped in conventions of publications and of scholarly debate, are less comfortable with pathways to knowledge that start with or refer to more anecdotal and idiosyncratic origins of learning.

Since one argument in these pages is that there is an imbalance in higher education between the power culture of knowledge-before-doing and the development culture of doing-while-learning, that particular advice - however logical - is declined. The author wants the medium to parallel the message. The chapter will start with the way we typically acquire its titular topic, tacit knowledge, by blending the serendipitous and the stochastic. First, the nature of the demand in development work will be briefly looked at, in order to provide a contrast with the way study programmes 'supply' knowledge for preparing people to practice it. By the end, two recurrent issues in HRD for development work will be focussed on; the question of relevance of training and the challenge of transfer of learning. Both can use a fresh framing, and the author will argue that tacit knowledge offers this. Oh, yes, and well into the text, I inform the reader what others say tacit knowing for development work is (i.e., I tell you what you will already know ...).

The 'demand' in development work

I want to set the context for our focus on knowledge acquisition for development work by referring to the recent dramatic economic miracle of the newly industrialised nations of the Far East. It is concluded in some circles that they owe their success to enhanced capital accumulation - not physical capital accumulation mind you, but human capital accumulation. According to a well known economist, this human capital accumulation - knowledge accumulation - is not from schools and R&D organisations, but from learning on the job. The distinctive characteristic of this knowledge enhancement in these export-led economies is its demand that 'workers should continue to take on tasks that are new to them' (Lucas, 1993, p.270).

This is a fairly startling conclusion for those in HRD (let alone possibly for economists!). An image ascends for me: if the most productive regional workforce in the world is always starting up new tasks in their work, this means they are always starting up their learning curves. Can it really be that millions of very productive people do not know all that much what they are doing? If so successful, what is it then they are so good at ..?

73

Well, one thing people in these newly industrialised countries (NICs) are good at is imitating and adapting their imitations in the light of experience. Like noviciates of yore who would sit at the foot of masters seeking to replicate the latters' core creative processes, these 'entrepreneurs (in the South) seek to mimic the production techniques developed in the North' (Grossman and Helpman, 1991, p.577). In economics-speak, this is called spillover, and is an example of Lucas' reference above to knowledge accumulation through on-the-job learning: '... many of the technical and managerial advances brought about by experience in the production of certain products ... (are) the result of spillovers from learning by doing in other industries' (my emphasis) (Young, 1991, p.371). Decades ago in a seminal paper in economics a similar argument was put forward: advances in technical progress - as well as emanating from think tanks and academic citadels formally designated to produce knowledge - were compared to a

> vast and prolonged process of learning about the environment in which we operate ... exactly the same phenomenon of improvement in performance over time is involved ... (this knowledge acquisition) can only take place through the attempt to solve a problem and therefore only takes place during activity (my emphases) (Arrow, 1962, p.155).

Here the word activity means productive work. It certainly does not mean, in the HRD sense, activity in a classroom, as in learner-centred activity or experiential exercises. What it means is economic activity, what Lucas called in his conclusion on the miraculous success of globally competitive economies, 'producing goods and engaging in trade'. Knowledge acquisition - 'the main source of differences in living standards among nations' according to Lucas - derives from the experience of work. Of course, Lucas tells us, 'human capital accumulation takes place in schools, in research organisations ...', but as the miracle story of the Far East serves as a reminder, 'little is known about the relative importance of these different modes of accumulation ...' A key choice then for Lucas is 'whether to stress human capital accumulation at school, or on the job' (1993, p.270). (For some growth economists the choice is clear: 'the accumulation of knowledge is the result of experience in production rather than a separate activity' (Stokey, 1988, p.702); and: 'It is the very activity of production which gives rise to the problems for which favourable responses are selected over time' through which 'technical change in general can be ascribed to experience ...' (Arrow, 1962, p.156).

The above observations, as well as setting a context, raise important questions in themselves for policy makers in HRD and economics, like whether workbased learning can sustain competitive advantage for the NICs if their volume of trade falls (as is happening at the time of this writing). Or whether a substantial investment to achieve a minimum threshold of formal education is needed before learning by experience becomes so economically productive as concluded above. Or to what degree the investment in formal HRD in Far Eastern societies is renowned for fostering outcomes in their workforces like creativity, adaptability and innovative thinking ... Here our task, though, is to denote from a learning perspective the distinctiveness of 'productive' development work. What is its characteristic demand developmentally?

An account of knowledge formation for industrial competitiveness in the highly successful Swedish offshore industry of mooring chains offers a starting point (Laestadius, 1995). A low tech company, Ramnäs Anchor Chains - what Drake (1995) has been tempted to label a glorified foundry - turns over some US$35 million or so annually in the immensely specialised, very tough market segment in mega chains. Ramnäs recently delivered the 'biggest order ever' of the 'strongest chain ever': 6,000 tons to the North Sea worth about US$20 million - over half its revenue for 1994. But since 1989, results at Ramnäs confirm its leadership in the industry, having

> maintained and even increased its market share in quantities parallel to raising its prices more than the competitors (reflecting a larger share of high quality shipments) (and) ... has also managed to increase its value added more than and to levels well above the average in Swedish manufacturing. (Laestadius, 1995, p.28)

This dramatic story of Northern European economic competitiveness owes its success to industrially relevant knowledge creation. But like in Southeast Asia and the Far East, this knowledge accumulation is not a function of formal education. Nor is it of company R&D, for at Ramnäs we learn that R&D accounts for less than 0.6 per cent of turnover and there is no reported patent activity. As part of a Swedish industry notorious as 'unskilled labour intensive', two thirds of its workforce have, at most, nine years of basic education; a quarter have one or two years more of vocational training. Two - only two - actually attended university. Ramnäs' formal competence is therefore 'very low' by average Swedish educational standards, let alone compared to the Swedish metal industry in general (Laestadius, 1995).

Yet, this company is consistently successful, highly competitive, a leading edge firm. Another image ascends: from where does this non accredited workforce derive its worldclass knowledge? What is this workforce so good at that allows it to meet so successfully its company's demand for continuous incremental innovation?

Well, one thing Ramnäs employees are good at is learning through the experience of working together. Underlying this 'development work' (Laestadius' phrase), the way of knowledge formation can be explained as 'an iterative process made economical and manageable' through minor and systematic variations on the shopfloor:

> Epistemologically this way of working comes close to what can be called an inductive methodology but the participants in fact have difficulties describing why they followed one way of reasoning instead of another. When interviewed they usually explained their creativity as 'experience'. Very little of all this incremental innovativeness and skill is documented. (Laestadius, 1995, p.30)

Could it be that a demand of development work makes it hard to say what you know of it? Do we have on our hands another paradox in HRD, where development work demands successful learning - learning which economically makes a difference, but which epistemologically leaves the learner feeling it does not. This contradiction in the characteristic of development work has been noted elsewhere: '... in many ways ... the very best kind of learning - that is why we often claim that 'learning from experience' or 'learning by doing' are the keystones of all real learning' - but difficult because it 'seems to drive out an awareness of learning' (Morris, 1991, p.175). So we have on our hands 'real' learning which cannot take place in the absence of development work, yet 'real' developmental work blotting out the real learning. At Ramnäs, the real expertise might be in calibrating the temperature peculiar to the second oldest Ramnäs furnace on a north facing wall, or fine-tuning the control of one of its welding machines to take account of infinitesimal differences in steel of the 'same' quality - but nonetheless in neither case the ability to articulate that expertise. Is this because people in such developmental circumstances become over identified with the subjective experience of tackling the demand of the work? It is as if they become at one with the work, making it hard for them to elaborate their skill. They become adept at doing something which transforms their relationship with their environment, yet the knowledge acquired in the accomplishment seems to dwell within them, making the productive process almost indistinguishable from them as producers. This leaves them taking their achievement for granted.

If we can generalise this as a characteristic in the demand of good development work, how might this relate to the way people are prepared to undertake it? From an HRD point of view, how would their training take account of this characteristic demand?

The 'supply' of development knowledge

> The normal approach in each session (of three hours) will be to begin with a lecture-type overview or introduction to the topic, and then to move into a more participative method, e.g., seminar discussion, case study analysis or practical group exercise as appropriate.

The above is from a course outline of a module in the MSc 'taught' programme in Human Resource Development and Human Resource Management at my University Institute. As an example of the anticipated use of a two-to-three hour postgraduate teaching session, the sequence outlined is probably pretty typical of postgraduate study in business administration, management and development studies up and down the land: presentation first by the tutor, followed by some class activity of the postgraduates. Lecture first: ensure the basic points get covered (but you can't lecture for three hours); so involve students next: some choice here (projects, tasks, groupwork, etc.). Yet this sequence in postgraduate HRD study strikes me in its emphasis as opposite to the characteristic extrapolated from the preceding section as a demand in development work. Indeed, in development work, people good at it are not able to say what they know of or do in it; but in postgraduate study for development work they must be able to say what they know - as must their lecturers who say it first. Of course at one level this is why we have in-service education and development training for practitioners in the first place: to enable competent, busy, practising adults to become better at learning what they know and do. I subscribe to that rationale for practitioner-oriented postgraduate study. But I am concerned that its dominant mode 'overrules', runs roughshod over, this aim.

The reliance on the twin chief modalities in higher education of listening to lectures and reading set texts orientates knowledge formation for the learner towards the knower (the lecturer or author) and towards the known (the publicised or published subject matter) and away from the postgraduate 'knowee' and the unknown. The logic behind this imbalance is unquestionable: this is known, we know it, so ought you. Mature students arrive in our classrooms in Manchester from overseas literally willing us to 'impart' our knowledge to them. As mature, experienced practitioners, they spend hours working alone at an abstract level to combine bodies of knowledge critically and make transparent the conceptual justification behind these intellectual syntheses. Again, on one level, this is a proper discipline in increasing one's professional competence as a practitioner - making evident the theory that informs one's practice. But is it the major task, given the social nature of the demand in practising development work? Is this emphasis in the supply of HRD provision - an emphasis I find increasing among academics forced to compress their teaching and inflate their publishing - conceptually justified vis a vis the demand in the practice of development work? If we were to paraphrase Laestadius from the previous section, we would be saying for success in the study of development work, 'Epistemologically this way of working comes close to what can be called a deductive methodology. The participants are accountable for making explicit why they followed one way of reasoning instead of another'.

So the provision supplying development knowledge - 'delivering' it is what our overseas postgraduates expect - seems to be inverting the characteristic demand in the development work itself. The implications of this inversion can be framed epistemologically by distinguishing between two types of knowledge. In doing this, I want to state at the outset I believe both types of knowledge are required for the practice of development work. My concern is with the theoretical justification of our provision: why 'supply' only one when both are 'demanded'? For some in academia a concern with the adequacy of theoretical justification must be threatening, for I find academics tend to hear the argument as one couched in either/or terms, as if only one kind of knowledge is being put forward at the expense of the other. But the real question is on what conceptual grounds do we favour the formation of one kind of knowledge and ignore the acquisition of another.

HRD for development work

Does contrasting explicit knowledge, the knowledge of formal education, with tacit knowledge, the knowledge of everyday expertise, help elucidate this HRD issue? Explicit knowledge is about what we know consciously (what we think we know). It is transmittable because it is symbolic. Postgraduate study is a cash transaction in this articulated knowledge. Academia is a wholesale outlet in it. But I contend development work trades in tacit knowledge. Tacit knowing is the embodied learning which competent doers have at their fingertips. When the sports star in the post game interview is asked to explain peak performance and more often than not replies something to the effect, 'I dunno. You can just tell when it happens,' that champion is tapping into tacit know-how. The illustration does not restrict a sports image to isolated technical achievements, like scoring a winning basket or goal. The metaphor of accomplishment in sport can parallel the reality of development work for it connotes complex social skills as well, like mobilising will in the face of adversity, taking risks under pressure or unfair conditions, and leading others by setting high standards in the face of incredulous odds or doubts. Tacit knowledge, therefore, also includes underlying assumptions and mental models rooted in a person's belief system and the implicit images of reality and of possibility they conjure up for the person. These constructs and theories-in-use influence a practitioner's intentions and actions immensely. If explicit knowledge is more about theory, tacit knowledge then is more to do with practice. The latter is the knowledge of experience, embodied through encounter, the former the knowledge of rationality, lodged in the mind.

While recent interest in tacit knowledge is largely focused on techno-logical innovation and transferability (Howells, 1995; Pisano, 1994), the differentiation of knowledge into tacit and explicit has been around for some time. The distinction appears from Michael Polyani's formulation 30 years ago of a tacit dimension in personal knowledge:

I shall consider human knowledge by starting from the fact that 'we can know more than we can tell'. This fact seems obvious enough, but it is not easy to say exactly what it means (Polyani, 1983, p.4).

Recently, an empirical enhancement to the contrast between tacit and explicit knowledge has been provided in Nonaka and Takeuchi's integrative theory of organisational knowledge creation (1995). Nonaka and Takeuchi find that tacit and explicit knowledge are woven through social processes in the organisation they call conversions, through which 'individual knowledges gets articulated and 'amplified'' (p.57). They find four conversions in successful Japanese businesses, as below:

- from tacit to tacit, a conversion they call 'socialisation'
- from tacit to explicit, called 'externalisation'
- from explicit to explicit, called 'combination', and
- from explicit to tacit, which they label 'internalisation'.

Their formulation is 'anchored to a critical assumption that human knowledge is created and expanded through social interaction between tacit knowledge and explicit knowledge' (my emphasis) and is 'not confined within an individual' (p.61). Importantly, they emphasise the second conversion mode above, externalisation: from their research into successful Japanese companies, the social conversion of tacit to explicit knowing holds the key to knowledge creation in organisations because this is where and how relevant new product and service concepts are generated. Their fourth conversion mode above, internalisation, is also particularly important to our focus on HRD in development work. This is because any change in development work only becomes developmental when the learning associated with the change becomes sustainable, when the development and learning transfer within and across the social unit or system.

So let us address these two fundamental knowledge conversions in HRD for development work: the conversion of tacit knowledge to explicit knowledge, which brings into consciousness the pervasive tacit knowledge of doing that we go on to combine with articulated knowledge, and the conversion of explicit knowledge back into tacit knowledge, which implants throughout the corpus the necessary knowledge of the mind that is needed to continue practice in the field. It will help in doing this to re-cap the four modes of knowledge conversion above, highlighting the two we are going to focus on by making their boxes (2, 4) bigger in Figure 5.1 below.

Now the two highlighted boxes above can be filled in with some illustration from Laestadius' case study, with an example each of these two chosen amplifications of tacit knowledge. Remember: it is through these two particular social modes of industrially relevant knowledge creation that tacit knowledge is exploited in the development work of a low tech firm in Northern Europe as well as in economically viable learning by doing in the Far East to maximise continuous incremental innovativeness.

Tacit to explicit, the second conversion mode of externalisation

An illustration of this conversion would be from the 'intensive dialogues' (Laestadius, 1995, p.29) between Ramnäs technicians and company suppliers of machinery. Ramnäs is what is called a 'demand former', shaping its subcontractors of equipment to improve. The result of this elaboration of developmental demand from the company is constant modification of techniques and the design of new equipment by suppliers. Sometimes this elaboration is informal, Ramnäs technicians' sharing ideas and problems, sometimes formal, with details specified by Ramnäs personnel.

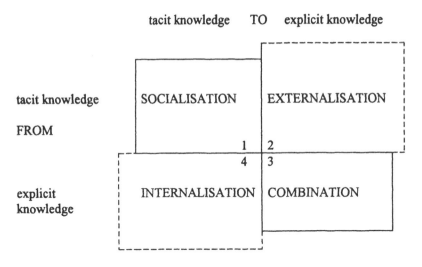

Figure 5.1   Four modes of knowledge conversion

Source: adapted from Nonaka and Takeuchi (1959, p.62).

Explicit to tacit conversion, the fourth conversion mode of internalisation

At Ramnäs this might be illustrated by the firm's role as an innovative 'demand receiver' (p.29). The ever rising standards of its high quality buyers and of classification companies like the American Petroleum Institute impel Ramnäs through their precise specifications to improve its own internal products and processes continuously. Ramnäs must translate these demands into new working practices and outputs among its employees. In this way recurrent improvement becomes normative.

Yet are not the knowledge conversions above through which tacit knowledge is mobilised for productive development work the very ones largely neglected in UK postgraduate study for development work? The dominant conversion mode in academia is that of explicit knowledge to explicit knowledge (more accurately, from the inference of your not having enough explicit knowledge, to 'acquiring' more of ours, in the form that we choose to supply it to you!). This of course is the third conversion mode, the one that Nonaka and Takeuchi call combination (see box 3 in Figure 5.1). That mode emphasises only the assimilation of different concepts into inclusive knowledge systems (like this chapter is trying to do). As Nonaka and Takeuchi say of knowledge combination, '... formal education and training at schools usually takes this form. An MBA education is one of the best examples of this kind' (p.67). But I wonder: by limiting the nature of their development programmes for master practitioners (MBAs, MScs in Management, MAs in Development Studies, etc.), do academic institutions inadvertently create two problematic challenges for themselves? One would be relevance in their training and the other transfer in their postgraduates' learning. The idea of knowledge conversion involving tacit knowing can help inform both. The issue of relevance in HRD programmes can be framed as externalisation, where tacit knowledge associated with development practice is required to be converted into explicit knowledge identified with academia. Transfer can be cast as internalisation: explicit knowledge that has been combined in formal HRD study is now converted into praxis for continued development work.

Relevance and transfer

The issue of relevancy in HRD study implies a relationship between course contents and their topicality in the development setting. Relevance is conventionally earmarked through timely provision of resources that make the subject matter resonate with the learner's experience. These include current case studies, credible speakers 'in the know' and fieldwork opportunities that parallel central issues in the development context (but with different detail). I have in mind in taught Masters' programmes short visits to organisations and projects, even to third countries, but basically 'looking-at-and-listening-to' guided presentations, not 'live-in' immersions or prolonged attachments. The conceptual justification behind efforts to make taught provision relevant is something along the lines that the relevant case or fieldwork offers a 'bridge' between what the lecturer knows ought to be understood and what she or he believes students ought to be able to understand. When such a bridge is constructed through relevant content, so the reasoning proceeds, it helps the postgraduate to consolidate what is being transmitted with what is to be assimilated. This is logical as far as it goes, which the reader will appreciate from a perspective on tacit knowledge is not far enough.

Why? Because teaching what is known - programmed, codified and syllabic - keeps the learning within but one realm of knowledge conversion, in this case, explicit knowledge combination. This 'supply' of development knowledge hardly meets the demand in the practice of development work because the learning is all deriving from a single thought world. The truth is that explicit-to-explicit knowledge formation can be emphasised as fluently when rubber necking in a Malaysian rice paddy on a study tour as when glued to a seat in a Manchester library, as elegantly through a Mauritian's lips in a smart lecture as from a Mancunian's. Simply relocating the mix of teaching explicit-to· explicit knowledge into or from another culture does not offset educational reliance on the dominant institutional mode of converting knowledge within the same paradigm. No matter how lively or contentious the classroom debate you produce or the reading list you set, mental exercise by postgraduates - irrespective of its robustness - remains a workout in box number three above, a conversion within the same kind of knowledge. But development work requires multiple conversion modes - 'more like a confrontation between different spheres (boxes!) of knowledge where 'what is of relevance in one thought world is not so in another' (Laestadius, 1995, p.31).

The challenge then is to bridge two cultures, not just connect or illustrate content within one thought world. And since the 'transformation from one thought world to another' is 'basically collective in character', the problem in relating the knowledge of the two cultures - the dominant culture of science, technology and education and the development culture of innovative practice and hands-on embodied learning - is 'large and easily underestimated' (Laestadius, 1995, p.31). To learn across paradigms as well as within one, postgraduates need learning opportunities from the outset that help them - in the scheme of knowledge conversion modes above - to shift within the second box, amplifying their tacit knowing through dialogue into explicit concepts and meanings, before they spend time articulating (in box 3) this coded knowledge. This would constitute a leap across thought worlds, and as a knowledge conversion signifies to me relevant knowledge acquisition across paradigms. Any number of academics reading this will say, 'What's new? Of course. We do this all the time, encouraging our students to share experience and provide starting points for discussion ...'

By lecturing first?

Transfer of learning in my experience is similarly regarded in too facile a manner. As a career HRD practitioner, I too have been concerned to 'integrate learning with work'. I periodically have gone through phases of attempting to reinforce learning after a course of study has finished. I confess supporting application within the workplace by a range of devices, from action planning to writing letters-to-self, the latter containing the learner's own handwritten reminders or pledges to take action later, sealed in a self addressed envelope at the end of training and then posted in two or three months to the practitioner.

But the very question of facilitating transfer and the very concentration on the accoutrements that accompany it are the manifestations of a thought world wedded to learning before doing. They are part of a pervasive syndrome, an institutional iatrogenic debility, of the culture of the classroom and the R&D laboratory which proclaims for development work inappropriately a drill of 'prepare first, perform later'. The continuing prominence of foundation courses in practitioner development is a case in point. Such structures imply that an actionable extra - actual practice - is optional, to be hived off from the prerequisite mental core. Such structures reveal an inadequate understanding of learning ability and knowledge formation in the applied behavioural and social sciences.

When learning is structured through the experience of productive work, however, it meets its own integral requirement for diffusion and transfer of knowledge formation. To paraphrase Revans (1971) then, there can be no productive activity without application, and no application without productive activity. The line of thinking of basics-first-followed-by-application-in-the-workplace erroneously 'assumes that the knowledge is already created, that the main intellectual work is done, and what is left is only a spread out. Our understanding of absorption ability and learning capacity', as Laestadius puts it, 'is not that passive' (1995, p.31). What can make it more dynamic is a perspective on the conversion of explicit to tacit knowledge. Internalisation of development knowledge is a knowledge conversion mode across paradigms. It is more like a consolidation between our different boxes of knowledge above and less like a before-after sequence within a single thought world. As something more complex than simply re-learning from the codified experience of another, it involves the re-experiencing of others' experience so that explicit knowledge becomes embodied as tacit expertise. It can never be simply absorbing mentally the previously articulated lessons of others. Like the challenge between thought cultures depicted in externalisation, the problems inherent in enabling internalisation should not be underestimated.

Nor should one underestimate the pervasiveness in development work in general of the dominant academic thought world. As Douglas has commented (did she have academics' manufacturing of explicit knowledge in mind and their trade in it in postgraduate programmes?), '... the whole process of entrenching a theory is as much social as cognitive' (1987, p.45). Academics themselves - true to the nature of knowledge conversion referred to in this chapter - go on to internalise their own entrenched theories, converting their articulated knowledge into tacit assumptions which they cease being critically conscious of. So when confronted explicitly with the notion of tacit knowing - as through this chapter - a typical reaction will be that tacit knowledge is not 'testable'. But sometimes the significance of something is more important than its testability. Cobblestones, Polyani reminds us, may seem more real than our trust in yet unthought of, untestable future ways, but compared with cobblestones our 'minds and problems possess a deeper reality ...' (1983, p.32).

Concluding remarks

Yes, the dominant cultural paradigm is alive and well and prodding debate - within it. My curiosity, however, is spurred to cross over its confines. I want us to break out of the ring of the single-paradigm thought world, to get out of what Nonaka and Takeuchi label as the Western mentality that thrives on the 'boxing of logic', with 'both sides being represented by explicit thinking' (1995, p.237). How long in higher education, then, will tacit knowing - and unorthodox means to elaborate it to strengthen capacity in development work - remain deviant and sub-cultural, a discounted anomaly on the fringe of a unitary thought world? Morris, who as the first professor of management development in Britain knows something about the challenge of legitimating development work within Western organisations, adds a note of caution: 'Much of the literature dealing with developmental failures reveals situations in which the two cultures (the dominant culture and the development culture) came into collision and, in the short term at least, the dominant culture won' (1991, p.182).

A final image descends upon me, driving home the depth of the difficulty behind the persistent discount of practical know-how by academic know-about. Dominik Cultah has just scored another early round knockout of Development Thought World: 'What a supreme victory!' the ringside presenter raves. 'Tell our viewers how you keep doing that, year in and year out?' A pause from the champ: 'I dunno'.

References

Arrow, K. (1962), 'The Economic Implications Of Learning By Doing', *Review of Economic Studies,* XXIV, pp.155-173.

Douglas, M. (1987), *How Institutions Think*, London, Routledge and Kegan Paul.

Drake, K. (1995), 'The Economics Of Learning On The Job: A European Perspective On Instruction-led and Experience-led Competence', paper presented at a conference on *Efficiency and Equity in Education Policy*, Canberra, 6-7 September 1995, convened by the National Board of Employment, Education and Training, and the Centre for Economic Policy Research, ANU.

Grossman, G. and E. Helpman (1991), 'Quality Ladders and Product Cycles', *Quarterly Journal of Economics*, 106, pp.557-586.

Laestadius, S. (1995), 'Tacit Knowledge in a Low-Tech Firm', *European Journal of Vocational Training*, no 6, pp.27-33.

Lucas, R. (1993), 'Making a Miracle', *Econometrica*, vol 61, no 2, March, pp.251-272.

Morris, J. (1991), 'Development Work and the Learning Spiral', in Mumford, Alan (ed.), *Handbook of Management Development*, 3rd ed Aldershot, Gower, pp.174-188.

Nonaka, I. and H. Takeuchi (1995), *The Knowledge-Creating Company*, New York, OUP.

Pisano, G. (1994), 'Knowledge, Integration and the Locus of Learning: An Empirical Analysis of Process Development', *Strategic Management Journal*, 15, pp.85-100.

Polyani, M. (1983), *The Tacit Dimension* reprinted Gloucester, Massachusetts, Peter Smith, first published 1966.

Revans, R. (1971), *The ABC of Action Learning: A Review of 25 Years of Experience*, Luton, Action Learning Trust.

Stokey, N. (1988), 'Learning By Doing and the Introduction Of New Goods', *Journal of Political Economy*, 96, 4, August, pp.701-717.

Young, A. (1991), 'Learning By Doing and the Dynamic Effects Of International Trade', *Quarterly Journal of Economics*, 106, pp.369-406.

6 Application of the learning theory in public sector: the case of decentralisation in the Philippines

Derek Eldridge and Ernita Joaquin

Introduction

This chapter demonstrates the application of recent developments in learning theory to a decentralisation process for public administration. The rise of concepts such as the 'learning organisation' and 'self organised learning' are shown to be significant ideas when addressing the learning domain of local government in the Philippines. Some of the stakeholders have already discovered the possibility of achieving the above through their own willingness to address change, their focus on local capability building and in instituting steps towards self-sufficiency in local development processes. As further experience accrues, it is suggested that the whole approach to learning for improved local government has to become more institutionalised. This process will also involve local government acting hand in hand with communities in discovering and learning about new possibilities in service delivery and resource creation. The role of training institutions will then become one of stimulating local government units to create an effective change process at all levels, as a replacement for standardised, off the job training courses for a limited number of officials. A major inference is that learning how to manage change at the local level is central to the whole concept of democratisation in the Philippines.

Background

When the Local Government Code of 1991 (Republic Act 7160) was signed on 10 October 1991 triumph mixed with apprehension, was felt at all levels of government, while the informed sectors of the population were immediately caught up with the excitement it generated. As landmark legislation under the democratic regime of President Corazon Aquino, the law promised the granting of meaningful local autonomy to the countryside.

Centralised governance of the country dated back to the Spanish colonial regime (1565), when the government established its seat in Manila. Early history of the sprawling archipelago suggests the existence of 'nation-states', with their own social, political and economic systems that were disturbed by the onslaught of foreign imperialism. Under Spain, the central government exercised authority through the provincial (provincias) and municipal/town governments (pueblos). The barangays (tribal villages) were consolidated under the towns. The only change in the structure up to the present time was the creation of city administrations.

The functions of the colonial central government included 'the supervision of justice, the collection of taxes, the maintenance of peace and order, the construction of public works, and the educational activities in the provinces' (Zaide, 1968, p.21). This introduction of a unified government is seen as having fostered national solidarity in the country. When the Americans assumed colonial control they retained the government set up, 'so similar to the old system as to be readily comprehensible to the natives' (Tapales, 1992).

Since gaining independence in 1946 various attempts at deconcentrating the government's administrative functions have been made, among them the Local Autonomy Act of 1959 and the Decentralisation Act of 1967. Deconcentration is also regarded as administrative decentralisation, is 'the redistribution of administrative responsibilities only within the central government' (Cheema and Rondinelli, 1983, p.19). The Local Government Code of 1983 consolidated all the laws pertaining to local government. But the local political system remained centrally bound, while a basically paternalistic culture ensured that financial control for local purposes emanated from the top.

Until 1991 legal measures all fell short of guaranteeing that the local developmental function could be pursued autonomously and potentially with adequate means. Thorough devolution was also regarded as political decentralisation, in other words, it was assumed that 'local governments have clear and legally recognised geographical boundaries within which they exercise authority and perform public functions' (Cheema and Rondinelli, 1983, p.22). The Code was aimed to operationalise this process by the provisions shown in Table 6.1.

Table 6.1
Decentralising for development under RA 7160

- strengthening the powers of local authorities, specifically of local chief executives, in 'area management', i.e. in local economic promotion and social development;

- devolution of the responsibility for the delivery of basic services (agriculture, health, environmental protection, social welfare) and regulatory functions from the national departments to the LGUs, including the projects and programmes in these sectors;

- devolution of management of national government employees, assets and records attached to the devolved services;

- an increased share of LGUs in national internal revenues, and their authority to generate locally-sourced incomes; and,

- an increase in the participation of the private sector and non-government and people's organisations (NGOs/POs) in local administration and development, by institutionalising their representation in key local planning bodies, and enhancing the mechanisms for collaboration with the private sector.

Operational issues in devolution

The Code's Implementing Rules and Regulations, were deemed to be of limited help as the various institutions attempted to implement their modified responsibilities. Associates in Rural Development's report notes that the:

prevailing conventional approach to cross-agency coordination cannot keep pace with the events, tends to exacerbate confusion at the local level and is consequently counter-productive (1992, p.3).

Constraints to a smooth development of responsibilities fell under four main headings:

The redeployment of centrally employed personnel

The transfer of personnel was hindered by a mistrust between the employees of the national departments on one hand, and the local authorities and employees on the other. For their part, local chief executives were wary of having to provide for considerable personnel expenditure, integrating the absorbed employees into the local government system, and consequently having to exercise new managerial approaches to deliver the devolved basic services. Governors and mayors were also concerned about gaining the loyalty of their new members, and risking division within the organisation between locally-hired employees and the devolved ones that could result from significant differences in status or compensation.

Redeployed employees, on the other hand, who received relatively higher salaries from the national government, were afraid that they would suffer from the budgetary constraints at the local level, as well as having insecure prospects for career advancement. In many areas, national employees resigned from the service rather than be transferred to local government control. Later on dialogues to reassure both parties were conducted, but only after mutual relations suffered an initial setback.

Inadequate information about the share for Local Government Units (LGUs) of the internal revenue allotment to finance the cost of devolution

Another burning issue that had persisted throughout the devolution discussion was the LGUs' mandated share from the Internal Revenue Allotment (IRA). The Code specifies that the IRA share of LGUs shall be allocated using a specific formula (see Table 6.2).

Table 6.2
LGU share from the national internal revenue

Allocating the share of lgus from the internal revenue		Distribution scheme per LGU for Provinces, Cities, and Municipalities	
Provinces	24%	Basis:	
Cities	23%	Population	50%
Municipalities	34%	Land Area	25%
Barangays	20%	Equal Sharing	25%

Source: Local Government Code of 1991.

The problem was how to appropriate the resources among the devolved functions, and to augment the amount if necessary. Provincial governments, which assumed the burden of personnel and service functions, for example, running the provincial hospitals, and feeling that the formula was unfairly biased against provinces, initiated legislative action to amend the formula through Senate Bills 284 and 285. Development advocates, on the other hand, noted that the distribution formula serves to reward highly populated LGUs. In addition, many complained about the allocation to cities which are cities in name only because of indiscriminate creation largely ignored by the national government in the past.

As LGU shares would depend on the level of national revenues and thus be limited, the pressure was on for local chief executives to learn to exercise the new powers aimed at creating additional sources of income and improving budgeting and financial management as LGUs implemented their devolved powers. Such efforts would have to overcome the initial perception that resource generation capacity at the local level was so limited that the national government might have no recourse but to keep on providing for an augmentation fund in the annual General Appropriations Act. This view has now declined, as evidenced by current developments manifesting local imagination in resource creation. For instance many LGUs nationwide have already enacted their own new tax codes and entered into development ventures with the private sector.

The sectoral orientation of national agencies contrasts with the area management of local governments

Some national agencies felt that their approach to service delivery contrasted markedly with that of local governments. It was quickly realised that the new relationship between national agencies and local governments should bridge this gap so as to learn new ways of providing services locally. National agencies would have to concede that public service should 'get closer to the public', and that LGUs may have a better insight on how it should be done including an ability to focus closely on supplier/client relationships. Centrally accrued experience in providing the services since the establishment of the Republic would need to be examined thoroughly and evaluated in a constructive manner, if it were to be of any benefit to the new providers of service. However, national agencies were somewhat reluctant to engage in such a process, in some cases, being fearful of revealing their own mistakes in service delivery.

In addition, strong reservations were expressed by regional officials of the Department of Health, backed by some local chief executives, about sustaining the delivery of health care services (Local Government Centre, 1994), the largest function to be assumed locally. As a result they were able to persuade some legislators to file bills extending the period of devolution, from one to five years (House Bill, 1476), or deferring the devolution of health care services to LGUs who elect for such deferment (Senate Bill, 1971). However, the necessary political will was mustered to proceed according to the original plan. These apprehensions could have been overcome initially if LGUs and national agencies had entered into a genuine, constructive dialogue to fully understand the new responsibilities and the support system that had to be set in place, 'rather than indirectly touched upon or avoided altogether', (Associates in Rural Development, 1992, p.7).

Resistance on the part of elected officials to NGO participation in local governance

One striking fact that emerged soon after the devolution was the resistance of many local elected officials to the election of people's representatives to the local legislative councils (the sanggunian), citing their irrelevance because, as they would have it, the incumbent female legislators already represent say, the women's issues. Although private sector representation in local special bodies, for example, health boards and school boards was facilitated by local leaders, some remained sceptical towards NGOs and POs occupying their allotted number of seats in local legislatures (at least 25 per cent of the total membership). In some instances, accreditation of NGOs and POs was marred by favouritism. This attitude also spawned the rise of 'fly-by-night' NGOs who could be identified by their political patrons, and who did not have solid records in development activities, and therefore should have been ineligible to participate in the selection. Nonetheless, much collaboration between the LGUs and the NGOs or the private sector has already been observed in development ventures.

Setting the scene for institution building

The radical nature of the code can not be understated. The majority have hailed it as epoch making. Within a unitary, presidential government system in force over a sprawling archipelago, the Code has devolved the role of providing basic community services from national agencies to LGUs, together with the human and material resources attached to this responsibility. In administrative terms this means enabling localities to determine their own paths to self-development by enlarging their financing powers and the avenues for people's participation in local government. Primarily however, it is enhancing the learning domain of localities by providing them with opportunity to consider three fundamentals in community building: their own willingness to change; the basis for local competency; and the ways of creating self sufficiency in development processes (see Figure 6.1).

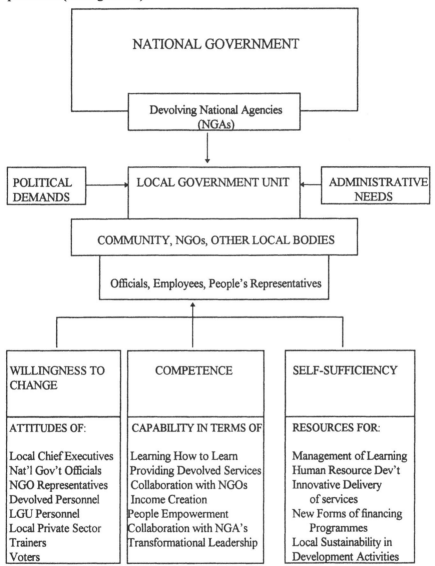

Figure 6.1 The learning domain of local governments

As LGUs began to assume these fundamental responsibilities, national agencies were urged to develop operational, hands-on manuals and other 'how-to' guidelines on the devolved functions, instead of just reiterating the general implementing rules of the Code. Subsequent administrative orders spelled a new role for the devolved agencies, especially for their offices in the field, aimed at facilitating learning by the LGUs on the nitty-gritty of the devolved functions, as well as helping them find their way about their new economic and social development roles, instead of burdening them with reporting duties. 'It is at this juncture in the decentralisation process that technical guidance from national agencies within the framework of local autonomy needs intense focus' (Associates in Rural Development, 1993). The phrase 'within the framework of local autonomy' stresses that national agencies are to support LGUs in their process of learning, instead of feeding them bureaucratic reporting guidelines.

There is thus a clear recognition of the need for building local institutions rather than maintaining them as adjuncts to central bureaucratic mechanisms, and for transforming their role to one of 'making local governmental structures and processes more responsive to the ever changing demands of the times' (Brillantes, 1994a. p.6). But further than just the realisation of a need to change it needs to be added that it has to be suggested how the change process should be enacted. In other words, the most significant and profound learning need of local governments at present concerns that of learning how to learn itself. Illustrative of this new found approach is that many local chief executives recognise the need for more demand-driven capability building strategies, away from the institution-based, generic management development and training programmes that have characterised capability building for so long (Associates in Rural Development, 1993).

Traditional reform in an LGU has usually focused on the training and development of top officials, without adequate recognition of the supporting role of the rest of the members of the organisation. Nor did it mention the need to upgrade competencies of the organisation as a whole within the context of its local conditions. While it is true that mayors or governors were trained on many matters, the programme content formulation was too centralised. The Local Development Assistance Programme, for instance, was a centrally organised training programme for treasurers regardless of the locality from which they originated. In general these programmes failed to consider varying local needs and to have an impact on performance. Moreover, training as an HRD strategy was often treated as merely another means for securing pecuniary/physical benefits in an impoverished economy. In contrast the new approach for devolution was seen to be addressing wider institutional aspects of change. For instance, at the close of the second year of the implementation of the Code, the Associates in Rural Development, Inc. (1993), noted that:

Transitional phase in the decentralisation process has thus begun. Local governments are turning to the substantive aspects of local control including reorganisation in the context of new responsibilities devolved to them, enactment of policies such as tax ordinances and zoning codes which enable local exercise of authorities, examining new methods of revenue mobilisation and, perhaps, most importantly, learning the essentials of delivering health, agricultural extension, social welfare, environmental and a host of other services for which they are now responsible.

Reconceptualising learning for development as implied by this quote encourages it to be viewed as a continuous and natural process, that is bound up with human experience and development (Smith, 1984). Whereas training may result in dissociation with the 'real' world, and often uses a prescriptive approach to problems, learning approaches to real and immediate problems keep people 'on top and on tap', to be always in a learning posture, flexible for change, and adaptable and responsive to the requirements of organisations (Varela, 1993). At the level of the organisation, the whole becomes greater than the sum of its parts as individual learning forms the building block of a 'learning system' as learning is a process that builds on itself. Learning 'is not the same as study, nor the same as training. It is bigger than both. It is ... a way of growing' (Handy, 1989, p.50). This kind of learning not only questions many of the assumptions traditionally held in regard to building local government capability, but also proposes some very challenging notions for individual and organisational growth - both for local governments and the entities (national agencies, training institutes) that have genuine concern for the development of local capabilities. It gives rise to the types of question shown in Table 6.3.

Fundamentally, the proponents of decentralisation from the legislature, the academe and the LGUs, in the Philippines, believe that, akin to the principle of Action Learning (Revans, 1983), LGUs will evolve from an attitude of dependence only when they are given full responsibility to rely on themselves. This will happen when they actually provide services, generate their own resources, and ensure the viability of local democratic institutions, and when they realise that no one else can do this for them. The granting of local autonomy automatically entails the expectation for LGUs to assume responsibility for building their own capabilities, but the preparation of the actors in learning skills is an essential prerequisite for this to happen. Local government training and consultancy institutions therefore have a new found role as stimulators of the necessary process skills.

Table 6.3
Areas for critical reflection in local government

Confronting the Questions of:

Willingness to change	The basis for local competency	Ways of building self-sufficiency in development
Is there a favourable attitude toward the principle of matching the rate of learning with the rate of external and internal changes?	How capable are local development actors in terms of:	How can the identification of existing resources, and the creation of new ones, be facilitated and supported by:
Are local development actors (LCEs, NGA officials, LGU employees, training providers, NGOs, POs, private sector partners, voters) open to new approaches to building capabilities for performing their new roles?	Learning-focused activities - learning how to learn - self-organised learning - people-empower-ment - transformational leadership - collaborative learning	the management of learning local HRD innovation in services, and productivity measures, Is it possible to build in a collaborative way a more sustainable local resource base, generating adequate taxes for local development.
Do we wish to encourage the development of questioning insight (reflective observation) in local government affairs?	Are there tools that we can utilise to engender continuous improvement?	

Establishing the scope for learning approaches

Decentralisation in the Philippines requires a fundamental change in the orientation of local governments, but one that does not leave them unaided in their search for new organisational purpose and the appropriate philosophical disposition in seeking out that purpose. Whereas superficially the problems appear only to be how to learn or perform their new functions, it has been shown that the change in environment is so vast as to question local capability, resources and attitude, in achieving decentralised development in the long term. A new approach to capability building is required if a breakthrough in current constraints is to be achieved. Changing the way we change, to use Cunningham's (1994) term, means learning to change the way we manage change. In learning organisations, (variously called learning enterprises, learning entities, or learning systems), individual members who are in themselves agents for organisational change, are also the agents for organisational learning. Along these lines, Argyris and Schon (1978) explain that:

> ... in order for organisational learning to occur, learning agents' discoveries, inventions and evaluations must be embedded in organisational memory. They must be encoded in the individual images and the shared maps of organisational theory-in-use from which individual members will subsequently act. If the encoding does not occur ... what individuals may have learned remains as an unrealised potential for organisational learning (p.19).

To build the organisational learning capacity 'about the interactions between the organisation's behavioural world and its ability to learn' (p.29), it is fundamental to have a process of organisational reflection and inquiry into the strategies for effective performance, the norms that define effectiveness, and what was done that facilitated or inhibited learning these. It is that critical process of 'encoding shared maps' in learning how to learn the 'area management' of Philippine localities that is central to institution building. Further, Argyris and Schon remind us that, '(a) process of change initiated with an eye to effectiveness under existing norms turns out to yield a conflict in the norms themselves' (1978, p.21). The search for newness is thus not only about level of output, but also for what local actors themselves believe are essentially a redefinition of local needs. For this to happen community/local feedback is essential. Also, managers as effective learners, need to be increasingly 'self-critical' of their own experiences as this primarily underpins the redefinition process of what local administration is going to be about in an autonomous context.

Already the relevant experience is being built as the local governments' 'learning curve is rapidly rising', as noted by the Local Development Assistance Program survey (Associates in Rural Development, 1993), while national agencies were urged to keep up the pace of providing LGUs with the technology and other support necessary to deliver the transferred services. In the same survey, however, remarks about the initial performance of LGUs as 'somewhat slowed down ... not as coordinated as before ... needing better organisation' (p.9) serve as a stimulus to make LGUs become fully cognizant of their new found role. Critical reflection is essential because giving responsibility to LGUs also involves the possibility that mistakes will be made. The question is what is the acceptable level of social cost in allowing learners to 'run their models' again, in the anticipation that the delivery of services could be improved the next time? This is, in part, a community question as well as a managerial dilemma.

People empowerment

There are some learning implications that can be identified with regard to the Code's provisions on an LGU-NGO partnership:

First, the work of NGOs, by definition, is grounded in approaches distinctly outside formal governmental structures and mechanisms. This means that NGOs have much to learn in functioning effectively within local government systems. In addition, NGOs and local authorities need to transcend issues of mistrust borne out of historical differences in orientation as far as development activities are concerned. For instance, the long period of authoritarianism in the Philippines under Marcos had spawned a 'leftist' image among NGOs that was seen by government functionaries as hindering participation (Brillantes, 1994b).

Secondly, community development as the traditional domain of NGOs has been supplemented with advocacy in areas of both national significance (agrarian reforms, foreign debt management, environmental issues) and sectoral scope, urban reforms, labour advancement, gender (Briones, 1992), issues not traditionally articulated by local government.

Thirdly, the existence of 'fly-by-night' NGOs and the stubbornness of local officials regarding sectoral representation in local legislatures (sanggunians) may have impeded collaborative learning between the two types of body.

For NGOs and POs who attempt to share their respective sectoral agendas with LGUs (on youth, women, fisherfolk, etc.), learning how to function within the framework of government requires skills in learning conversations in order to negotiate with local officials in setting development targets. Their traditional advocacy roles may make them feel constrained by the existing parameters of government (structure and legal context), but they will need to learn how to collaborate primarily within them. At the other end of the dialogue, political leaders are required to transcend issues of mistrust and a feeling of superiority over people's representatives. As mentioned, they should be able to share maps of organisational 'theory-in-use' and subsequently act from them, bearing in mind that effective learners constantly find that others do not necessarily share their own views. Given the natural disinclination of NGOs to political strategies, especially in the Philippines where local power-play has for so long been blamed for rural backwardness, identifying and negotiating common concerns could become quite an effort. It is the reason why learning conversations should be sustained and managed in meetings between two parties.

Within the context of such partnership both sectors need some 'retooling' or to develop their capabilities in order for them to recognise and appreciate the nuances of each other's unique cultures (Brillantes, 1992b, p.584).

They also need to face up to the idea that change through collaboration involves a number of risks. The types of issue to be faced are these:

1. In collaborating with LGUs in the management of change, and in ensuring that accountability is observed by local institutions (of which some of their own peers are members), could the community (financially) afford learning from mistakes?
2. If outcomes from shared purposes and strategies are negative, how much support can people lend to the learning process? What does this imply for community awareness, local politics and the management of resources?

At the heart of these issues lies a concern about how public learning can 'convert anxiety and hostility' at the grassroots level into 'a creative form of energy' to help produce leaders who learn rather than leaders who merely perform. It is the power of the people themselves that provides the inspiration for LGUs to learn effectively and also provides the ultimate judgement on how much has been achieved in this respect.

In methodological terms the type of learning response required of the wider community is somewhat more strategic in concept. So far we have discussed the learning process in terms of the support dialogue or conversation between parties to jointly achieve new levels of competence. This more strategic concept involves a referent dialogue (Harri-Augstein and Thomas, 1991, p.133) by local people to learn how well local government has built its capacity and performed. It is the level of learning about how the LGU has learned. It recognises that '(being) able to express an intention is not equivalent to achieving it' (p.134); that, having established the purposes for certain local government ventures, people can either:

1. learn to anticipate outcomes of the directionalities over which one has no control, i.e. acknowledge the LGU's limitations and learn to make the most of what it can do ('passive purposefulness'); or, better yet,
2. by committing public support not merely because of expected positive outcomes, but to the overall process, they can help control the direction of

change, alter strategies, revise original purposes, and achieve true, 'active purposefulness'.

Self sufficiency for local development

The controversies that have surrounded the distribution of the LGUs' share in the national internal revenue merely highlight the hitherto paternalistic nature of the relationship of the national government towards local affairs. In order to reduce the dependence of LGUs on central funds and to sustain the delivery of basic services, various income creation methods are allowed by the Code, such as:

- local taxations;
- credit financing: deferred payment, bond flotation, inter-local government loans and, financing the construction, maintenance and management of infrastructure projects by the private sector through the Build-Operate-Transfer (BOT) scheme;
- 'market decentralisation' schemes: deregulation, local investment promotion; and,
- economic enterprise development.

Some of these mechanisms are already being undertaken by the more innovative local government units.

However, most LGUs are still 'novices' when it comes to creating their own sources of revenue to finance development programmes. They have generally lacked creativity and have not had enough authority in the past to engage in economic activities, apart from managing poor-performing public enterprises and utilities such as public markets, slaughterhouses and the like. Also they have had little political will to install and maintain a credible system of taxation, thus creating an attitude of dependence on the Manila-based government. An effective learning approach would seek to remove this attitude of dependence and inspire the creation of a self-sustaining local tax base including new financial ventures.

In this respect, two cases that may be considered are those of the Municipality of Muntinlupa and the City of Olongapo. In the former, the new Code has allowed Mayor Ignacio Bunye to push through a plan to utilise credit facilities for road and waterworks schemes, which has been hailed by the wider community as showcasing a 'high sense of business appreciation' (Joaquin, 1994, p.36). For the latter, when the source of employment of the skilled local workers disappeared with the removal of the American naval presence, Mayor

Richard Gordon led a core group of selected people who came up with the idea behind what is now the Subic Bay Metropolitan Authority, a Hong Kong type freeport using the abandoned facilities which has now attracted investors worldwide and become 'a symbol of the country's economic re-birth' (Parrenas, 1994, p.52).

No doubt many more cases of successful experiments are now being taken and they will need to be identified to feed the wider learning environment. In particular, these illustrations lead us to ask of leaders in learning conversations: how were they able, in collaboration with their colleagues, the private sector, clients, and citizens, to 'model their jobs', to understand what was appropriately required of them? How is the change from a dependent into a self-sufficient LGU achieved in an autonomous setting? How did they appreciate the objectives of entrepreneurial governance using, or without being constrained by, the legal framework to serve the best interests of the locality, which may well illustrate Cunningham's point:

First order change is change within defined and accepted parameters. It is about incremental change, which is often doing more of (or better than) what we have done in the past ... Second order change occurs when we move outside existing parameters and frameworks. It can mean changing the way we change (1994, p.29).

Learning does not necessarily mean going only for grandiose results as these initial examples suggest, but that significant re-thinking is needed if only to eliminate wastage and fiscal misappropriation in the public sector. If 'response to feedback is the way learning takes place' (Senge, 1990; Ashridge Management Centre Paper, 1990), how is learned change to be conducted when feedback of the following type is common?

... the persistent problem of low (tax) collection efficiency is attributable not just to an unimaginative treasurer, but to a whole institutional environment that fosters the idea that a 50% collection rate is 'normal', (Associates in Rural Development, 1993b, p.25).

Many of the questions we have asked about people's participation can also be directed at this issue. Can we measure learning in the area of generating income as we do it, not only after tangible outcomes (financial statements, income accounts) have been reported? At a corporate giant, IBM, the chief executive officer is reputed to have said that '(our) business is learning and we sell the by-products of that learning' (Pedler, et. al., 1989, p.4). Carrying this perspective into the public sector would be a challenging task for leaders in convincing their constituents that learning how to make communities economically self-sufficient takes time, and that costly mistakes could happen in the process.

Conclusion

In the foregone discussions the learning issues that underpin moves to make capable and self-reliant communities possible have been identified. The means, however, by which these needs can be met is the issue of learning itself, compared to which the other needs are ends in themselves: we are referring to learning how to learn as a primary tool of decentralisation and transformation.

Learning how to learn as a concept is bannered by several philosophies - Self-organised Learning, Action Learning, and Experiential Learning - all of them grounded on the assumption that access can be made to 'a lot of resources within us with which we had lost touch', (Harri-Augstein and Thomas, 1991, p.341), resources largely available that can allow us to better come to terms with human needs. Attempts have been made to demonstrate how the underlying principles of these philosophies fuse into a powerful doctrine of learning, so dynamic it guarantees to turn individual as well as organisational activities into endless, stimulating, learning events. However, it is beyond the scope of the present discussion to detail these methodologies and indeed, it may be inappropriate at this juncture. Picking up the process of learning is a responsibility of the stakeholders, including the choice of appropriate methodology, although local training institutions may wish to advance their views on this issue.

It is concluded that decentralisation and its implicit goals - competence, self-sufficiency, and a willingness to direct change at the local level - could prompt people to question whether and how they are exploring their inner capabilities to learn as members of communities contributing to local development. There are indications that it is already happening, but that there is a need to structure that experience. Can local chief executives alone be entrusted with the responsibility to initiate and oversee this structuring of the whole process of learning? Senge argues that:

Our traditional view of leaders - as special people who set the direction, make the key decisions, and energise troops - are deeply rooted in an individualistic and non-systematic worldview ... Our prevailing leadership myths are still captured by the image of the captain ... leading the charge to rescue ... At its heart, the traditional view of leadership is based on assumptions of people's powerlessness, their lack of personal vision, and

102

inability to master the forces of change, deficits which can be remedied only by a few great leaders (1990, p.340).

A deeply patriarchal society fostered by Spanish colonisation, has reinforced these myths in the Philippines, consigning responsibility to men of status rather than allowing for the realisation of the potentials of people to learn for themselves. In the modern workplace, the proponents of self-organised learning, Harri-Augstein and Thomas (1991), declare that:

> ... the organisations in which we work are built on ... myths which assume us to be the other-organised receivers of consequences not of our making. Our implicit models of such situations are built up unknowingly to contain such assumptions as threats of redundancy, job changes and re-training, environment changes ... new technology in the home and at work and so on, but at the explicit conscious level we are encouraged to believe ourselves to be autonomous (p.337).

This incompatibility between the implicit and explicit models, between the appearance of controlling and being actually controlled, according to them, produces much of our individual frustrations. With decentralisation there is, we believe, the capacity at local level to ensure a genuine autonomy which is not just another incompatibility at the macro level. There is evidence that already there are local chief executives in the Philippines who underlie their Codal functions with an aim to overhaul this state of incompatibility. They are several examples of leaders, who, surpassing the role of a captain in charge of a helpless party, and choosing not to control them, derive satisfaction from seeing that people do learn for themselves.

Recently, analysts have noted the trend toward dynamism in the Philippines amongst governors and mayors, whose age range is considerably lower than that of their predecessors, and whose lineages do not necessarily show political history in them. It has seemed more and more that the feudalist mode of local politics has a hope of being transformed to produce what Sosmena (Local Government Centre, 1994) brands as the 'third-generation' (local) leaders, not merely orientated to welfare and relief policies, nor imbued with the principles of development administration, but with the ability to become leaders and advocates in an ever-complicating environment and to constantly stimulate community learning.

References

Argyris, C. and D. Schon. (1978), *Organisational Learning: A Theory of Action Perspective*, Addison-Wesley Publishing Co, USA.

Ashdridge Management College Management Skills Group. Book Summary No. 13 (1990), on Senge, P. *The Fifth Discipline: the art and practice of the learning organisation*, Doubleday, New York.

Associates in Rural Development, Inc. (1992), *Rapid Field Appraisal of the Status of Decentralisation: the Local Perspective*, Local Development Assistance Program, Manila.

Associates in Rural Development, Inc. (1993), *Third Rapid Field Appraisal of Decentralisation: the Local Perspective*, Local Development Assistance Program, Manila.

Brillantes, Jr., A. (1994a), *Reinventing Local Government Management in the Light of the Local Government Code: a perspective from the Local Government Academy*, paper presented at the National Conference of the Association of Schools of Public Administration, College of Public Administration, University of the Philippines.

Brillantes, Jr., A. (1994b), 'Redemocratisation and decentralisation in the Philippines: the increasing leadership role of NGOs', in *International Review of Administrative Sciences*, 60(4), pp.575-586.

Briones, L. (1992), 'Decentralisation, Development and the Role of Nongovernmental Organisations', in Lim, J. and Nozawa, K. (eds), *Decentralisation and Economic Development in the Philippines*, Institute for Developing Economies, Tokyo, pp.207-246.

Cheema, G. and Rondinelli, D. (1983), *Decentralisation and Development: Policy Implementation in Developing Countries*, Sage Publications, London.

Cunningham, I. (1994), *The Wisdom of Strategic Learning: The Self-Managed Learning Solution*, McGraw Hill, London.

Handy, C. (1989), *The Age of Unreason*, Business Books Ltd, London.

Harri-Augstein, S. and Thomas, L. (1991), *Learning Conversations: the self-organised learning way to personal and organisational growth*, Routledge, London.

Joaquin, M. E. (1994), *A Case Study of the Local Government Code Implementation in Muntinlupa, Metro Manila*, Local Government Centre, College of Public Administration, University of Philippines.

Local Government Centre (1994), *Integrated Terminal Report on the National Conference on Local Autonomy, Decentralisation and Development*, College of Public Administration, University of the Philippines, Diliman, Quezon City.

Parrenas, J. C. (1994), 'The Philippines in the Next Six Years', in *Progress Through and True: A Vision for Philippine NIChood*, Centre for Research and Communications, Manila, pp.50-57.

Pedler, M., Boydell, T. and Burgoyne, J. (1989), 'Towards the Learning Company', in *Journal of European Industrial Training*, vol. 20, Part 1, pp.1-8.

Republic of the Philippines, *Local Government Code of 1991 (Act 7160)*.

Revans, R. (1983), *The ABC of Action Learning*, Chartwell-Garatt Ltd, England.

Senge, P. (1990), *The Fifth Discipline: the Art and Practice of the Learning Organisation*, Doubleday, New York.

Smith, R. (1984), *Learning How to Learn*, Open University Press, England.

Tapales, P. D. (1992), 'Devolution and Empowerment: The 1991 Local Government Code', in *Philippine Journal of Public Administration*, 36 (2), pp.101-114.

Varela, A. (1993), *The Role of Local Government Executives in HRD*, Lecture presented to the 36th Course of the Local Administration and Development Program, College of Public Administration, University of the Philippines.

Zaide, G. (1968), *Philippine Government*, Modern Book Co. Inc, Manila.

7 Training and transfer of learning: international dimensions

John Launder

Introduction

The transition from 'learning' to 'doing' may well be the most crucial and most neglected phase of training problems (McGhee and Thayer, 1961).

It may seem obvious to suggest that training needs to be seen as a means to an end, and therefore to be judged on its outcomes rather than purely on the training process. However in most training situations which involves off-the-job courses, the problem of effective transfer of learning back into the work organisation is often not well considered by the trainers, the sponsors who fund the training, and the student's employers. 'Positive transfer is often expected to happen automatically, as an inevitable consequence of formal learning processes' (Analoui, 1996, p.1). This can ignore the realities of the workplaces to which students return after training, where the social, cultural and management aspects of an organisation may facilitate or frustrate transfer of learning.

Transfer of learning can be a particular problem for students from developing countries who have attended Overseas Training courses in industrialised countries (OT), since the social environments and resource endowments of their home organisations may be very different from the context of their learning. Also, the problem of transfer of learning can even be perceived as a greater problem when the training itself has a high social dimension, such as in management, where new skills and styles of management learnt on courses may be difficult to implement in the social environment of the returning student's employing organisation. Overseas students' work organisations are likely to be more hierarchical and bureaucratic, such that innovation may be difficult to implement.

There is potential for programmes which combine an overseas training course with a practical training event in a third (developing) country, and which by so doing improve the transfer of learning through a training experience which is more proximate to the students' own situation. It is sometimes argued that training of developing country students is more effective in terms of transfer if the training is in another developing country rather than a industrialised country. However, students and employers still show very strong preferences for training in industrialised countries. The combination of OT and Third Country Training (TCT) can meet both those preferences and the need to promote more effective transfer.

There are also specially commissioned programmes for particular organisations where overseas trainers can visit the group of students and their organisation prior to the overseas course, for a better understanding of the potential for transfer of learning. Then later visits with training events can further assist the process of transfer and also evaluate the effectiveness of the programme. In order not to confuse it with another system, this could be called the 'Visit and Train' model.

The Development and Project Planning Centre (DPPC) at the University of Bradford has had experience with both these kind of training programmes. These have included various management courses and courses in agricultural project planning. The latter can be seen as essentially a 'consultancy' type of work, for which project planners need both technical and social skills for the collection of information from a variety of different people (from ordinary farmers to senior policy makers), as well as skills and knowledge for design and analysis of projects.

This chapter begins with looking at the scale of overseas training of students from developing countries, and the problems of evaluating that training. It then considers a social-technical model of training which can be adapted for the case of overseas training. Various case studies from DPPC's experience are considered and broad conclusions are reached.

Evaluation of training and transfer

There is potential for training to achieve a great deal, but the presence of transfer problems may mean that in some cases training actually achieves very little in terms of actual improved performance of the student's organisation. While OT is costly, relative to TCT and In-Country training (ICT), the capacity to effectively evaluate OT is problematic.

In 1987 the OECD countries spent $1140 million of bilateral aid to fund 110,000 scholarships for overseas training; in 1988 the UK spent over a hundred million pounds on 13,000 training awards. It is estimated that total bilateral and multilateral aid for overseas training was running at $1.5 billion at the end of the 1980s (Action Aid, 1990, p.5).

For evaluation of the real effectiveness of training in terms of transfer of learning the problems can be argued to be twofold. Firstly, it is difficult to differentiate a) the effect of a training course on a student's abilities from b) the effect of the social and organisational factors in the student's workplace on their capacity to apply their new knowledge and skills. Social and organisational factors may aid or nullify the transfer and application of learning. Secondly, with OT, the distances and costs involved in effectively evaluating transfer of learning some time after an overseas course may be prohibitive on a student by student basis.

In practice, it appears that there are differences between claims for high rates of return from training on the one hand and lack of substantive evidence on the other. Mingat and Tang (1988) reviewed many World Bank projects and concluded that project related training can have high rates of return, but this depends on various conditions such as education levels and infrastructure. They also found that agricultural project related training can have relatively higher returns.

Conversely, Action Aid's interpretation of Robert Cassen's influential 1986 report 'Does Aid Work' was;

> that most evaluation in this field (aid to training) remains qualitative and that many judgements are based on educated hunches rather than substantive evidence. (Also) evaluation of training ... is a topic about which objective data is hard to collect; inputs are dispersed among a wide number of transient individuals receiving training from a variety of providing agencies; effects and impacts are experienced in thousands of agencies in hundreds of countries, after considerable and varied time lags, and are part of a chain of events contingent on many supporting factors (1990, p.13).

Action Aid (1990) also reviewed a number of the UK Overseas Development Administration's (ODA) evaluations of UK OT but found the results to be limited and often inconsistent. However, the evaluations did indicate;

- a common complaint of lack of practical content in OT courses,
- higher relevance (and lower cost) of third country training,
- need for support on implementing learning from OT into workplaces,

- and: 'the impact of training individuals is often limited because when they return to their work they are unable to implement their learning' (ibid p.34).

Estimation of rates of returns on education and training programmes often uses a method of comparing different lifetime earnings between trained and untrained persons, by assuming that earnings reflect an economic value of work. However, given the problems associated with transfer of learning, transient students, and the reward systems of public services, it is unlikely that the above assumption holds. Hence such rates of return may be significantly overstated. A real evaluation of training and its transfer must address the problem of differentiating between the effects of the training and other reasons for improved performance. In the longer term, the World Bank believes that a major way to improve training effectiveness is civil service reforms which improve management systems, but acknowledges that evaluations of these efforts have not reported much success so far (World Bank, 1994).

For all training, and especially for management and project planning (consultancy) training, there is a need for trainers to acknowledge and address the process of transfer of learning within the training course itself. Trainers have various techniques for this, including simulations and action plans, and programmes can include post-course projects prepared by students after they return to their workplaces. More comprehensive and more effective options are training programmes which combine OT with TCT, or Visit and Train programmes, and these are explored in more detail following a discussion of some models of training and transfer.

Socio-technical models of training

It is argued that understanding the problem of transfer of learning requires distinguishing between the 'technical' and 'social' elements of the learning process. Technical aspects relate to the knowledge and skills required for tasks, while social learning relates to the complex of social, cultural, institutional and management structures which exist within students' workplaces (Analoui, 1993, 1996). These social structures may include various management styles, under which innovation may be encouraged or discouraged; industrial relations in terms of personnel management and restrictive practices; and hierarchical or bureaucratic structures versus more participative or team approaches.

Training on-the-job takes place within these social structures and relates job tasks and skills directly to such structures, hence the transfer of learning is accomplished simultaneously with the training itself. Training courses away from the workplace are generally considered more appropriate for learning of more complex knowledge or skills, having the advantage of less distraction and more concentration, and less disturbance to workplace operations. But this kind of training then has to face the problem of transfer of knowledge and skills back into the social structures of the workplace.

According to Stammers and Patrick (1975), transfer of learning;

occurs when the existence of a previously established habit or skill has an influence upon the acquisition, performance or relearning of another habit or skill. 'Positive transfer' occurs when the existence of the previous habit or skill facilitates learning the new one; 'negative transfer' refers to the interference by a previously learned habit or skill on new learning (p.96).

This can be interpreted as suggesting that the habits and skills previously developed in the social structure of the workplace influence the extent to which new habits or skills can be firstly learned and secondly applied. For example, students from highly bureaucratic organisations may have problems with learning and applying participative management styles; students from strongly socialist countries may have problems with learning and applying concepts of commercial operations in market economies. These habits or attitudes relate to both the students and to their workplace managers. In practical terms, the more the off-the-job trainer knows about the students' workplaces and their managers then the better they can design training courses which promote transfer of learning.

Models developed by Analoui (1993) show how the effectiveness of transfer of learning is observed to increase as the proximity to the workplace increases, while the effectiveness of learning more and more complex knowledge and skills increases with lack of such proximity. It is proposed here that Analoui's general propositions can be extended to international dimensions (see Figure 7.1 and Figure 7.2).

In the international context In-Country Training (ICT) has the greatest proximity to the workplace, and would be expected to have the highest effectiveness of transfer of learning. Whereas OT, with the least proximity, is often preferred for training in the more complex knowledge and skills

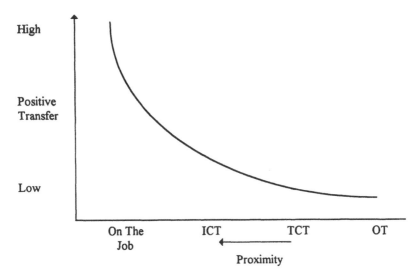

Figure 7.1   **Effectiveness of transfer of learning in relation to workplace proximity**

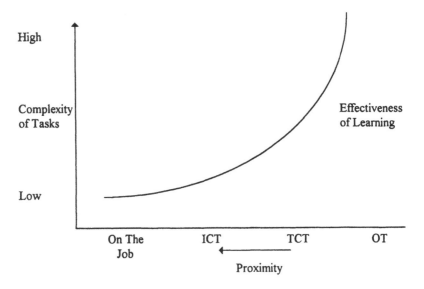

Figure 7.2   **Effectiveness of learning in relation to complexity of tasks and workplace proximity**

areas. With TCT having medium proximity, the continuum could be seen as:

ICT...............TCT (Regional.............TCT (Non-Regional.............OT (Industrialised
    Developing Country Developing Country)   Country)

For example, for a Zambian student, the continuum could be:

Zambia.................Kenya.............................India...............................Britain

In this international context, there are additional social and cultural factors involved when travelling to foreign countries for training, with the problem of transfer increasing as these additional socio-cultural differences increase.

And, these differences in socio-cultural factors between countries are all the more important in terms of training when the skills and knowledge to be learned and transferred also involve high social skills and knowledge content as in management and project planning/consultancy training.

Clearly, the various training locations have advantages and disadvantages, which are summarised in Table 7.1.

One fundamental training method to aid both the learning and its transfer which can be attempted in almost all off-the-job situations, is that of incorporating elements of simulation of the students' home workplaces into training courses.

According to Stammers and Patrick (1975);

Fidelity of simulation usually refers to the degree of realism or the degree of representation of the real task by the simulator' and 'Stimulus Similarity: When a task requires the learner to make the same response to new but similar stimuli, positive transfer increases with increasing stimulus similarity' and 'Increasing degree of fidelity usually implies increasing cost of simulation (p.96).

In OT courses in management and project planning/consultancy, trainers can use classroom techniques involving participation, role plays and case studies to try to simulate the problems and socio-cultural situations of students' workplaces. This will probably be simpler to run for single-cultural groups. In multi-cultural groups the variety, of say management styles, of different cultures may sometimes inhibit learning; but on the other hand the cultural diversity of the students may facilitate exchanges of experience which address fundamentals of common problems. Also, use of

Table 7.1
Advantages and disadvantages of OT, ICT and TCT

Partly by reference to Kerrigan and Luke (1987, pp.68-181),

OT advantages:	Exposure to new ideas and experience Sharing comparative experiences Cross-cultural exchanges Prestige, upward mobility on return English language competence enhanced
OT disadvantages	Lack of relevant simulations of home conditions Lack of opportunities for practical fieldwork Costly in foreign exchange Permanent losses of trained manpower (brain drain) Negative cultural assimilation e.g. consumerism Prestige may distract from choice of best training
ICT advantages	Relevance and proximity for transfers of learning Close links possible between on- and off-job training Low cost
ICT disadvantages	Lack of training resources Narrower curricula, reliance on formal methods Lack of courses for specialised and senior training No exposure to comparative experiences
TCT advantages	Can select regions with proximate simulation Comparative experiences Less cultural assimilation and collision than OT Medium cost
TCT disadvantages	Lack of training resources except in few centres Lack of facilities for receiving foreign students Complex administration e.g. visas, air travel.

some early team-building events can strengthen group socialisation, address culture differences, and attempting to make the classroom a temporary workplace with a unique social structure of its own.

Clearly the better that trainers understand the culture and problems of different countries the better they can design training simulations. However despite all these efforts to simulate students' home situations, and address cultural diversity, the real problem of transfer of learning by an individual student depends on what they are able to do on returning to their own organisation.

The actual workplace ... plays a determinant and decisive role in either 'making or breaking' the objectives (of) training programmes (Baldwin and Ford, 1988, p.38).

Better OT programmes, aiming to maximise effective transfer of learning, would include preparatory visits by trainers to students' workplaces, identifying together with students and their managers the training needs in terms of both the technical and social aspects of students' work, and then devising a training programme which complimented on-the-job training and ICT; included managers' commitments to a structured period of re-assimilation of the student into their workplace after their OT; with eventual evaluation by overseas trainers and managers of both training and transfer of learning some months later.

Examples of this kind of programme have happened with DPPC courses commissioned for particular groups from similar organisations in one country, when DPPC trainers did visit trainees and their managers both before and after the training in UK.

However, this is not a feasible option, in terms of cost and time, for courses which draw students from a variety of organisations in many different countries. For these courses a more feasible option is the combination of an OT course and a TCT practical training event, in which there is greater proximity to students' home workplaces, and the capacity for more practical simulation of their home conditions. Both training and transfer of learning can be potentially more effective from a well designed OT plus TCT programme, compared to a purely OT course.

Development and Project Planning Centre experience

In the last few years the Development and Project Planning Centre (DPPC) has built up experience with various programmes using the above models of

OT plus TCT and Visit and Train. These are summarised below, with further details following.

1. Bradford courses for international groups in Agricultural Project Planning followed by practical workshops in a third country (OT plus TCT).
2. Programmes for Indian Commercial Public Enterprise Management training included workshops in India both before and after the course in Bradford (Visit and Train).
3. A programme for Bangladesh Women into Senior Management included both pre- and post-course workshops, plus a visit to a third country (Visit and Train plus TCT).
4. A Kenya Senior Administrative Officers' Programme, including pre- and post-course workshops, with visits to various third countries (Visit and Train plus TCT).

International courses in agricultural project planning (APP)

In 1994 and 1995, two-month courses in Bradford on Agricultural Project Planning and Analysis were followed by Field Workshops of three weeks in Kenya. Numbers were small with four Trainees in each year, although in 1995 the workshop was joined by four Kenyan students. The workshops were based at the Kenya Institute of Administration (KIA) near Nairobi, with fieldwork arranged with the local administration of Machakos District.

The objectives for the workshops were that the students would investigate a real project proposal in the field, and prepare a Pre-Feasibility Study Report. This would be a practical consultancy task, with data collection, interviews with farmers and officials, data analysis including financial and economic analysis of the project, and report preparation. Finally the students would make a presentation of their report to the Machakos District officials.

Each year the students succeeded in producing a useful project report which was appreciated by the Machakos officials. (In 1995, the report produced in 1994 was an actual working document for the project, which had gone ahead.)

From evaluations at the end of both the workshops, the students agreed that the main training objectives had been achieved, and that there was much in the experience that they should be able to apply on returning to their organisations. Also, in terms of the workshop reinforcing the training at Bradford, the workshop was also rated a success[1].

In terms of evaluation of actual transfers of learning, attempts by DPPC to contact the students for their evaluation of this did not succeed; no questionnaires were returned. This demonstrates the problem of evaluating the transfer of learning when dealing with an international group, when visits to students after a course are not a viable proposition.[2]

In terms of proximity and simulation, the 'consultancy' nature of the workshops seemed to be a success, in a way which would not be possible in the UK. The relative social and technical homogeneity of the international group of students, gained from their previous interaction and training in Bradford, helped them to gain much in both the social and technical dimensions inherent in the consultancy exercise.

Indian commercial public enterprise management programmes (CPEM)

This Visit and Train programme was conducted in 1995 and 1996. It was designed for combinations of senior managers from Indian public corporations and senior government staff. The programmes were intended for the trainees to study strategic policy and management issues within their organisations and to learn about UK experience in public enterprise reform.

The twelve month programmes started with workshops in India, with the DPPC trainers visiting in order to identify training needs with students and their managers, and to agree on the research projects which were a key feature of the programmes. The second legs were the courses of two months each in Bradford, which included training in policy analysis plus organisation and management. Six months later, the trainers returned to India for workshops where students made presentations on their projects, '...to demonstrate application of their learning in their implementation in the workplace' (DPPC, 1996).

Bangladesh women into senior management programme (WISM)

This programme can be classed as a combination of Visit and Train and Third Country Training. It included a twelve week course at DPPC followed by two weeks in Malaysia, which involved exposure to models and experiences of senior women in the Malaysian public service. The designated DPPC trainer was able to visit Bangladesh before the UK course, and again the following year to evaluate the transfer of learning. While all but one of the trainees had changed jobs, all had been promoted, and all reported that the training had increased their effectiveness, and their organisation's effectiveness. Particular mention was made of increased 'confidence to plan and implement managerial procedures and skills acquired through training' (Amos-Wilson, 1997). The students' managers confirmed that their competence had increased, and also in comparison to others who had not had such training. The third country training in Malaysia was reported as very useful, and particularly for the cultural facet of meeting 'other Moslem women there, who had developed strategies for dealing with problematic issues at the workplace, within an Islamic context' (Amos-Wilson, 1997).

Kenya senior administrative officers programme (SAOP)

This long running programme (1989-1995) also can be classified as Train and Visit plus Third Country Training. The annual programmes included prior workshops in Kenya, a course and study visits in the UK, and visits to administrative institutions in various third countries. The model had;

> a core concept (which suggested) that senior officers should not be 'trained' (but) should be 'exposed' to good practice in a number of countries, ... transfer it to conditions at home ... (however) its effectiveness as a training method supposes a number of prior conditions ... these conditions did not always exist (Cusworth and Watson, 1995).

As a result, the last SAOP, while adhering to the basic concept, contained a number of innovations: more emphasis on management development through analysis of lessons from exposures and their implications in Kenya, management of change in a reform context, and use of action plans and follow-up workshops.

The final 1994 programme and the transfer of learning from it was evaluated in a workshop in Kenya in 1995. While need for further evaluation of transfer of learning was recommended, participants reported a 'major impact' on their work 'which exceeded expectations' and of 're-orientating their management styles towards one that is based on 'facilitation' rather than 'direction' (Cusworth and Watson, 1995).

The above examples all represent attempts to enhance both training and the transfer of learning. However they are quite different in terms of clients and approach. The CPEM, WISM and SAOP were programmes, designed for a particular client group's objectives, formulated as a 'project', and with definite finance from a sponsor (British Council). On the other hand APP had none of these features. The students had a variety of jobs, came from various countries and organisations, and had different sponsors for their training. The training programme of OT plus TCT had to be 'marketed' internationally in competition with other OT courses, and largely financed by the students' fees from a variety of sponsors. APP was a pilot project, involving elements of risk, and in the event DPPC lost financially.

From this experience, the Visit and Train model has obvious advantages over the OT plus TCT model as exemplified by APP. The former a) includes trainers' prior familiarisation with students and their organisation, b) can establish a programme of OT, ICT and organised transfer of learning, c) can also include third country experience, d) facilitates evaluation, and e) is less risky for the OT trainers.

On the other hand, the key feature of the APP type of internationally open OT plus TCT model is that individual students from many countries can have the opportunity to enhance their transfer of learning by the combination of an overseas course with a third country training event. While the elements possible in the 'visit' part of the other model cannot be expected, the gains from the proximity and simulative aspects of a third country workshop after an overseas course should provide substantial gains in terms of transfer of learning. If this is accepted, then the challenge for the training institutions and the sponsors of students is to work out suitable scholarships and funding arrangements.

DFID and training

As noted earlier, the UK Department for International Development (previously ODA) spends in the region of a hundred million pounds annually on training awards for students from developing countries.

The ODA also has addressed many of the above issues in its 1992 document 'The Power of Change' (ODA, 1992). It includes the premise;

> ... training is part of a wider set of objectives and not an end in itself ... training does not simply consist of attendance on courses; it is a multifarious activity that includes on-the-job training, study visits, management consultancy exercises, action research and distance learning (ODA, 1992, p.5).

Among other things, the Power of Change generally advocates more use of TCT, although it accepts that training courses in the UK will continue to dominate in its training programme. The Power of Change is also partly a response to the Action Aid report which found that despite 15 years of advocacy in ODA of more TCT, 'there is little evidence of efforts to utilise third country training more extensively, except in the SADCC region'

(Action Aid, 1990, p.56). In the mid-1980s OT accounted for 95 per cent of training awards, with TCT between 4 per cent and 5 per cent (ibid, p.22).

According to the Power of Change, important advantages claimed for TCT include greater relevance, especially for field experience training, cost savings, and institutional strengthening. Disadvantages include administrative problems, and monitoring and evaluation (ODA, 1992, p.9).

Concluding remarks

There are essentially two stages to training, the training or learning itself, and the transfer of that learning into the trainees' workplace. Then, within training there are two dimensions, the technical and the broadly social, with the social, cultural and institutional factors of the workplace largely determining the extent to which students can transfer their learning into improved personal and organisational performance. Transfer of learning is not an automatic process, but an issue to be addressed in the design of training programmes.

This is especially true for trainees from developing countries attending overseas training courses, when those social, cultural and institutional differences are that much greater. Very large sums of money are spent on overseas training, and it is the preferred option for most trainees and employers, yet it is difficult to evaluate the extent to which organisational performance increases after training.

It has been argued that, however good overseas training courses themselves are, the actual performance of returning students can be improved by various ways of addressing the issue of transfer of learning. For a start these can include simulation exercises within the training course itself, distance learning or project work before and after the overseas course, and greater contact between trainers and employers.

However the issue of transfer of learning can be more directly addressed by the proposed models of 'Visit and Train' and 'OT plus TCT'. Of these, the Visit and Train programmes have distinct advantages in terms of familiarisation by trainers of students' workplaces, follow up and evaluation, and administration and finance. However, the model is not viable for courses recruiting individuals from many different countries, when the model of an overseas course followed by a practical workshop in a third country can aid transfer of learning with increased proximity and simulation of the students' home situation.

Finally, training programmes which are specifically designed to promote transfer of learning are especially relevant to subjects like management and project planning where social and institutional aspects play a large part.

Notes

1. The Course Director of the 1994 course and workshop said in his own report: 'we are convinced ... that as a result of this experience, these study fellows are the best trained agricultural project planners that DPPC has produced' (MacArthur, 1994).
2. Before initiating this programme DPPC expected that students from Asia would not be attracted to a workshop in Kenya. In fact, over the two years nearly half of the students came from Asia, made no adverse comments, reported a high level of satisfaction with the training, and expected to use the knowledge gained in their home workplaces.

References

Action Aid (1990), *The Effectiveness of British Aid for Training*, Development Report 1990, Chard UK.

Amos-Wilson, P. (1997), Report on Follow-up Visit, Women into Senior Management Programme - Bangladesh, DPPC Bradford.

Analoui, F. (1996), 'A Socio-Technical Framework for the Effective Transfer of Training' *New Series Discussion Papers No. 70*, Development and Project Planning Centre, University of Bradford.

Analoui, F. (1993), *Training and Transfer of Learning*, Avebury, Aldershot.

Baldwin, T.T. and Ford, J.R. (1988), 'Transfer of Training: A Review and Direction', *Personal Psychology*, 41, pp. 630-705.

Cusworth, J.W. and Watson, J. (1995), Kenya SAOP Final Report on Follow-up Workshop, DPPC, Bradford.

DPPC (1996), Course Report: Commercial Public Enterprise Programme, Bradford.

Kerrigan, J.E. and Luke, J.S. (1987), *Management Training Strategies for Developing Countries*, Rienner, Boulder.

Launder, J. (1995), Course Report, Agricultural Project Preparation Field Design Workshop 1995, DPPC, Bradford.

MacArthur, J.D. (1994), Course Report, Agricultural Project Preparation and Analysis 1994, DPPC, Bradford.

McGhee, W. and Thayer, P.W.(1961), 'Training in Business and Industry', in Analoui F., *Training and Transfer of Learning*, Avebury, Aldershot.

Mingat, A. and Tan, J-P. (1988), *The Economic Returns to Project Related Training*. In Watson, K 1993; 'The Power of Change - A Response', Occasional Paper 1, UK Forum on International Education and Training, Birmingham.

ODA (1992), *The Power of Change*, Overseas Development Administration, London.

Stammers, R. and Patrick, J. (1975), *The Psychology of Training*, Methuen, London.

World Bank (1994), *The World Bank's Role in Human Resource Development in Sub-Saharan Africa*, Operations Evaluation Study, World Bank, Washington.

8 The new public administration - new challenges for development and implications for the development training institutions

John Cusworth

Introduction

A chance remark made by a senior official of a major bilateral aid donor at a major international conference organised by the Commonwealth Association of Public Administration and Management (CAPAM) in June 1996 provided the origin for the present work. This was to effectively question the relevance of sound development project planning processes and procedures in the context of what may or may not be a new paradigm in public administration. Perhaps this rather innocent and even correct observation would have probably gone unnoticed were it not for the background context of the conference, its theme and more importantly the source institutions of some of the participants.

The conference theme was predominately geared towards re-inforcing a view that a decade of public sector reform, headed by the UK, New Zealand and one or two other old Commonwealth countries had resulted in a new paradigm governing the role and function of the sector which should now be exported to other parts of the world and developing economies in particular. This being seen as complementary to and consistent with more general economic reform programmes aimed at liberalising these economies. The purpose of this chapter is not to discuss the validity of this view, or even whether there is such a thing as the 'new' public administration. Rather it is to discuss what the implications are for development assistance and for the traditional providers of development studies education and training. It might be helpful however to briefly summarise what the new paradigm involves as a way to highlight and preface the issues.

The new public administration

This brief summary draws heavily on papers presented at the CAPAM conference by Mohan Kaul and Nick Manning from the Commonwealth Secretariat. Kaul's paper is included along with others delivered at the conference in the February issue of Public Administration and Development, Volume 17, No 1.

It is perhaps useful to illustrate the nature of the new public administration by comparing the characteristics of what might be called the old public administration and the new. The old assumed that the public sector was the principal vehicle for securing socio-economic development (Gillis, 1980). The all prevailing role of the state in guiding development, in part fueled by the ideology of the eastern block, and heavily supported by western development assistance which was principally managed on a government to government basis, gave rise to the common phenomena in developing economies whereby government controlled practically everything (UN, 1975). In India this was explicitly referred to as the government controlling the 'commanding heights' of the economy. The reform programmes introduced in many developing economies may have scaled down this process but generally government is still seen as the main vehicle for guiding the development process even if not quite so directly (Narayan, 1994).

Other major characteristics of the old public administration is the emphasis given to stability and continuity combined with a strong commitment to maintaining law and order. This is further re-inforced through a strong sense of loyalty to the powers that be. Innovative thinking and maverick behaviour is not encouraged. Members of provincial and district administrations in Africa and some parts of Asia appear to have inherited these characteristics from their colonial masters with little by way of adaptation.

Such characteristics are reflected in the organisational structure of the old public administration which is dominated by Weberian hierarchies (1964). Handy (1981) describes such hierarchies as having a predominantly 'role' based organisational culture in which the accent is on routinised administration and systems maintenance. The old administration might also be characterised by what Hofstede (1980) termed a high power distance relationship in which the hierarchy is structured in such a way as to ensure that access to the centre of power and influence is limited and heavily formalised. It is also likely to be characterised by what Rondinelli et. al., (1990) refer to as a routine mechanistic management style which is unresponsive to its environment and primarily aimed at avoiding risk and uncertainty.

In contrast the new administration is generally considered to be target and objective orientated having a decentralised, team based organisational structure. In organisational culture terms it would be characterised by a 'task' culture with the emphasis on achievement as opposed to maintenance (Handy, 1981). Standards and targets are set and performance appraisal is a central part of the managerial process. Ability to deal with change and innovation, and a capacity to manage uncertainty are characteristics of this 'adaptive' style of management as Rondinelli defines it.

The focus is also supposed now to be towards the 'customer'. No longer are people the public, patients or passengers - but customers! (Ouchi, 1981). Presumably the idea being that the public sector no longer exists just to look after the people who work in it but to actually provide services to the people who pay for them in a more direct and accountable way. This is supplemented by a greater transparency and availability of information often associated with the use of information technology. Above all the new public administration is supposed to have a much greater emphasis on 'value for money' and cost effectiveness (IDS, 1990). Whilst there must be serious questions as to whether the new approaches are truly more cost effective than the old, as we who now spend our lives preparing project proposals must ask, advocates of the new order are convinced they are.

In looking at the summary characteristics of the old and the new, and in taking into account the trend towards smaller government through privatisation it does suggest that there may be a new paradigm governing the management of the public sector (Cook, 1988). But irrespective of whether there is or not the main point as far as this discussion is concerned is that it does appear as if many people and institutions believe that there is something genuinely new and that they appear to be turning it into a product which can be sold and exported. To some extent there is nothing new in this. The more developed nations have always considered that exporting their best practice was a good thing. But is there something more fundamental happening which will have major implications for development studies training institutions.

Emerging alternative approaches to promoting development

In a fast changing world no one can reasonably argue for the status quo and it is inevitable that new ideas and approaches in all fields will be developed. In terms of socio-economic development many new initiatives have been introduced over the past decade or so. The emphasis has been broadly focussed around getting macro economic instruments and policies right in order to stabilise economies and create the conditions for growth within a free market private sector based system combined with investment in human resource development involving a focus on health and education. Lessons from the SE Asia tiger economies are broadly adopted. However given the relative lack of effective government and other institutions specially in parts of Asia and sub-Saharan Africa these approaches have also involved continued technical assistance for the development of institutions generally within a framework designed to support democratic governance, a reduction in the size of the public sector and an increase in its effectiveness.

It is this latter point which is of relevance to this discussion. As Kaul points out the new public administration involves re-thinking the role of the public sector. This goes beyond the rather simple test question of should this or that be the responsibility of government or the private sector which could be defined as purely an ideological question without reference to economics or managerial effectiveness (Cook and Kirkpatrick, 1988). It also relates to the manner in which the public sector is run. It is this view which has possibly signalled a major shift in development circles in the UK and elsewhere which is now beginning to impact on UK providers of training, research and technical assistance.

Given the received wisdom that the new public administration is working based around privatisation, next step agency development, contracting out, compulsory competitive tendering, target and performance assessment etc. it is reasonable to expect donor countries to assume that the new approach to be major means to overhauling moribund, corrupt and undemocratic state institutions in developing economies (Lau, et. al., 1980). There are however several equations that stem from this assumption.

As indicated above one is the fairly fundamental one of whether or not the new approach really does give rise to the benefits claimed for it even in the countries where it has been developed. It is perhaps too early to really answer this question although there is apparently evidence to support opposing views on the issue. What is clearly less certain is whether the approach is transferable to other less developed economies which do not have developed private sectors, have relatively weak democratic government and lack robust institutional frameworks. To say nothing of masses of poor people living in uncertain and resource poor circumstances with no formal social security mechanisms.

However assuming for the moment that the approach does deliver the benefits claimed for it and that it can be fitted into the context of developing economies, there remains the issue of how best to transfer the approach.

126

This is where the question arises as to whether this process of transfer is now a major new approach to development in itself. Are we seeing the development of an approach to development assistance based around the main practices and procedures which underpin the new administration? If government reform and institutional development programmes can be seen as the major vehicles for delivering this transfer then their very existence in such programmes almost everywhere would indicate that the process is well under way. Perhaps of interest in this respect is who and what institutions in the donor countries are involved with the process.

The new providers

For the best part of three decades of human resource development for promoting economic and social development in UK development studies centres have played a major role as provider of education, research, training and advice. Their strength has been an ability to work with donors and the local institutions based on an understanding of the contextual framework of developing economies generally developed from first hand experience. They were also able to apply a critical perspective on practices and procedures in an effort to bring about improved approaches. Whilst these strengths still exist the issue is whether they are relevant to government reform programme based round the new public administration.

The higher education sector in the UK is not itself yet widely perceived as being part of the new administration. Whilst individual centres may have coped with the introduction of market testing in day to day operations their parent institutions are not yet perceived as being fully up to speed with the new approaches. The Research Assessment Exercise and Teaching Quality Assessment are clearly part of the new process it might be argued that the higher education sector is one of the last sectors which have yet to undergo dramatic reform. Jobs for life, rigid pay structures, archaic promotion procedures and an apparent resistance to change tend to characterise the University sector. It is hardly likely therefore that sponsors of government reform programmes incorporating the transfer of the new approach to public administration would automatically look to the university sector for training and advisory work. The fact that academics are by definition likely to be critical of supposedly new concepts would also make them unlikely protagonists of measures which are driven more by ideology than as yet proven economic or managerial effectiveness.

If the traditional providers are not then the most appropriate people to turn to for promoting the new approach who would be. One source of expertise would be the more traditional public sector training providers.

Given that these have been heavily involved in training for the UK public sector they naturally have relevant experience. The UK Civil Service College is a good example of such an institution and it is noticeable that they are now very much more active in developing and transition economies. Some of the other more mainstream business schools which have provided management training for the public sector are also now much more active in these areas.

Outside the formal management training institutions there are also now very many private providers of public sector management training. Many are individual consultants or groups of consultants which include people who have been heavily involved with public sector reform. Donors such as DFID have made extensive us of such people as key advisers and consultants. Another source of provision to assist in the process of transfer is of course the reformed institutions themselves. In order to operate the new system effectively there has been a need to invest in the human resource of these institutions, not just in the new practices and procedures necessary for their implementation but also in the wider ability of the workforce to manage the process of change. Local government departments, health trusts and even the utilities are providing courses and attachments on a commercial basis as are a few former government departments now turned into agencies. For example the former Agricultural Development and Advisory Service, in its guise of ADAS International, now offers a wide range of advisory and training work abroad and particularly in eastern and central Europe. Even the British Council made an albeit ill fated attempt to develop an active training section in direct competition with the traditional providers of training whose services it previously only managed.

It could be concluded therefore that the 'new' administration has led directly to the development of a range of new providers in the development arena. Agencies which are formed through the process of reform behave entrepreneurially and branch out into new areas in order to survive. Furthermore they are bound to be perceived by aid managers as more relevant for use in 'transferring' the new approaches overseas as they are themselves direct products of the process.

Implications

Perhaps in many ways the shift in development assistance towards an emphasis on good governance and government reform and away from more traditional investment in productive and infrastructural sectors has come at a bad time for some traditional development training centres, although conversely it may also be beneficial to others. It is a bad time because of other factors affecting them such as the fall out from the Power of Change, the general cuts in the DFID budget and in particular the disproportional cut in the budget for training.

At the extreme we may be seeing the end of an era. Most UK development studies training institutes grew up on the backs of the post colonial period in which the UK was required to service the needs of the UK aid programme and to maintain a cadre of expertise to continue this into the future. This direct linkage has long since gone although their was a belief in some quarters that perhaps there was still a recognised need for their existence in places where it mattered. Few people really believe that this is the case now. The fact is that opportunities for young professionals to work in development are diminishing. The new managers of the aid budgets are increasingly people with little or no front line development field experience and who have been brought up in the new culture characterised by the emphasis on 'value for money'. This gloomy perspective could ultimately lead to the dissolution or radical re-structuring of some institutes. This is clearly a fundamental challenge to many of them. At the moment the UK still has a comparative advantage in being able to offer research, training and consultancy in the field of development studies which is the envy of other countries. Once this is dissipated it cannot readily be recovered.

Conclusion

It remains to be seen whether the advent of the new public administration and the economic reform programmes across the world will ultimately lead to the demise of the traditional development studies training capacity in the UK or whether it can adapt to change and continue to play an active role in assisting in the process of development.

References

Cook, P. (1988), Economic Liberalisation, Privatisation and State Enterprise Efficiency on Less Developed Countries, report to British Council/Overseas Development Administration, September.

Cook, P. and Kirkpatrick, C. (1988), *Privatisation in Less Developing Countries*, Brighton, Wheatsheaf.

Gillis, M. (1980), 'The role of the state enterprise in economic development', Social Research, Seminar.

Handy, B.C. (1981), *Understanding Organisations*, Penguin, London.

Hofstede, G. (1980), *Cultures Consequences*, Beverley Hill, California, Sage.

IDS (1990), 'Profit related pay', An IDS study, December.

Lau, A.W; Newman, A.R. and Broadley, L.A. (1980), 'The Nature of Management Work' in *Public sector, public administration*, mimeo, No.40, Sept./Oct. pp.513-520.

Narayan, J.L. (1994), 'Implementation problems of public sector planning in less developing countries: a comparative analysis' in F Analoui (1994) *The realities of managing development projects*, Avebury, Aldershot.

Ouchi, W. (1981), *Theory Z*, Addison Wesley, Reading, Mass.

Rondinelli, D; Middleton, J. and Verspool, A. (1990), *Planning education reform in developing countries*, Duke University Press, London.

United Nations (1975), 'Development Administration: current approaches and trends in public administration for national development' New York.

Watson, C. (1977), *Managing Development through Training*, Addison Wesley, London.

Weber, M. (1964), *The Theory of Social and Economical Organizations* (Translated), Glencoe, Free press.

9 Experiencing the experience of small groups

S. Tene Kaminski

Introduction

Attempts have been made, in this chapter to conceptualise emotion as a two-tier system of perception, communication, cognition and motivation which is triggered to protect the self image of reality when challenged, or projected in order to create an image of reality, externally on others.

Emotion perceptions are used to determine individual and group reactions to new stimulation, either in response to experiencing new situations, or to discrepancies in previously encountered situations.

Emotion proper is a high-level unconscious or instinctive response, while feelings or moods are consciously constructed responses to previously experienced stimuli, emotion at the lower level is capable of being socially constructed, while high-level emotion is not, rationality is only maintained at the low-level.

Theoretical basis

According to Czarniawska-Joerges (1993), the purpose of academic referencing can be 'a historical, or in place of, or as a counter argument, or apolitically, or a shopping list of authors, clearly ... a list of names is not a text, it is by definition a list, i.e. a set of discrete elements. The value of such lists is informative and inspirational in order that the trail can be followed by others with similar or divergent interests.

The concept of emotion as a two-tier system is based on the distinction that Jung, (1977), made between emotion and feeling in his first Tavistock lecture. To Jung, emotion was the unconscious response to stimuli which involved physiological changes, while feelings are conscious constructions.

For McDougall, (1946), emotion was instinctive responses to stimuli, Bion, (1996), invented the terms, 'valency', and the 'proto-mental system' in order to account for emotion perceptions in his group work and also used Kleins, (1990), concepts of 'projection and transference', Katz, J (1980), developed her theory of 'discrepancy', to account for the triggering of emotion responses in previously encountered situations.

Rorty, (1980), writes of the 'interwoven strands of perceptions' of which emotion forms a part, according to Bowles, (1994), organisations have a 'shadow side'. This paper argues that this shadow side is the side which manipulates the subjective emotion perceptions of groups and individuals in order to achieve organisational goals. This manipulation is the cause of stress within organisational members who, in addition to performing their work for economic gain, exchanging their physical labour and energy, are also being required to perform 'emotional labour' (Hochschild, 1983).

The subject of the transference and projection of emotion energy formed part of the content of papers by Letiche and Van Mens, (1996), who dealt with these projections onto people, and Glinka and Lukaszewicz, (1996), who dealt with projections onto artefacts. Freud (1966), has noted the 'tendency to symbolisation develops early in life' and Walter (1968) that 'meaning means association'. It appears therefore that the association of meanings with symbols provokes emotion perceptions and responses in individuals and groups.

Goffman, (1971), describes 'primary and secondary adjustments', in the context of this paper, a primary adjustment would be a high-level response to stimuli, while a secondary adjustment would be a constructed response to a previously experienced contextual stimulation. Emotion would in Jungs', (1923), terms be the way we 'feel into' reality and as Gagliardi, (1990), who after discussing the role of 'Logos and Ethos' as components of culture adds 'pathos, the way we perceive and feel reality and its representations'. In other words the way in which emotion associates meaning with action and behaviour.

As Rokeach, (1960), states in belief systems, which are after all built on providing meaning through associations, 'It's not what you believe that matters, but the way you believe'. And as Bion, (1996), found, it is not what is said in the group, but the way it is said, for emotion perceptions detect discrepancies between the words and the behaviour.

Background

The Trans-European Management Conference is an annual event held each year at the Kolping-Bildungsstatte, Coesfeld, Germany, the 1996 conference took place between 22-29 June.

The working hypothesis of the conference is that new realities in politics and business mean that we face new realities in the future. We therefore need to be aware of how we experience these realities. The conference would give us insights into possible new personal and organisational realities.

The methodology is based on the idea that the truth about ourselves is revealed by experiencing different realities. The conference forms a temporary learning system which creates an environment with space for the delegates to broaden their understanding of these new realities, and which the delegates can use to expand their horizons.

The conference is comprised of six events, this paper is the ethnography of one of those events the International Event (I.E.). This event allows the delegates to form groups based on language or nationality, focusing on the experience of groups working together, the conference plenary sessions stated that, 'because of environmental changes the role of management is also changing, we are here to 'experience the experience'.

The method is for us to interact with realities and gain experience beyond the normal frame, to challenge our fantasies and illusions and to prepare for emotion and feelings, focusing on what it means to be a manager.

The aims of the conference are to provide learning experiences and opportunities and to check our understanding of working across national boundaries, and our social interactions. Our roles will involve spiritual linking of human beings with the environment and working across systems, the rationale is to experience and learn, the consultants will provide the hypothesis and the experience.

Incessantly we are taught that what really matters is the experience gained here and now, (Glinka and Lukaszewicz, 1996).

The dragons of Coesfeld

An ethnography of the international event

This event comprises six one hour sessions with a plenary sessions at the end for the groups to present their findings to the whole conference. There were six groups located in six separate rooms with a consultant assigned to each room, we were first warned of the procedure paradox then allowed to form our groups.

The consultant for our group was Ann Barry, the members were, Alexandra Schmidt, Dorota Anna Siemieniecka, Dr Frank Behrens, Ingor Dierkes, and the author. The topic of discussion was provided by Alexandra, it was leadership. The name was agreed by the group members at the start, and this was the only group to have a name in this or any of the events. It was the smallest group in the event, and the language used was English.

The group by nationality comprised of three Germans, one Pole, and one English. However one of the Germans had a Hungarian grandmother, and the English member was half Polish. By sex there were three males and two females.

The delegates had all previously been assigned to the small session groups and the role analysis groups by the consultants. This was the first event when the delegates could choose their group members. Two of the members of the dragon group had already by coincidence, or synchronicity been assigned together in their small session group, and they subsequently worked together in five from a total of six events over the eight days of the conference. The only group they did not share being the role analysis group. They of course formed a dyad, as Laing, (1969), states 'only if two people carry out reciprocally successful acts of attribution can any genuine relationship between them begin'.

International event, I.E. plenary session This is the international language event aimed to build groups. Several of these groups formed quickly, and left the conference room. To a certain extent the dragon group was formed from the people left behind, but then again, as the groups formed and left, the individuals which formed the dragon group had had the opportunity to join these groups but for whatever reason they did not join them.

I.E. small sessions - 1430 - 1530 hours and 1600 - 1700 hours The group spent the first two sessions discussing leadership in general and the relationships and relevance of leadership for countries and nationalities. We discussed national stereotypes and myths, also the socio-economic aspects of leadership and power.

The group also discussed what other nationalities thought of our countries which involved each of us defending our own countries and cultures from the myths and stereotyping we had discussed earlier. Although four of us were from the EU, Dorota was not, and we all tended to assume that the EU was Europe until Alexandra reminded us that the EU was not the whole of Europe.

This then led the group to discuss the images we had of winners and losers, in the context that the winners are the leaders while the losers are the followers. In this context western Europe are the leaders in social and economic terms, and as a result also in political terms, while eastern Europe are the losers, hence the followers.

The group also discussed if a nation had a personality or character based on their culture and beliefs, and how what we where discussing was relevant to the group name. The group pondered if size was relative to leadership, were different attributes required to lead a small team, organisation or a country? The group decided that the principles where the same regardless of size.

The group also considered if leadership involved managing ambivalence, it did. We ended the second session by deciding that we should keep a record of our group in order to present a paper of it's activities and findings. This paper is based on the notes taken during, and immediately after the group sessions, and of course the author was given the role and task of writing the paper. The group decided that it would experience leadership by exercising leadership in order to define what leadership in Europe means.

I.E. small sessions, Monday two small sessions, plus an additional one and a half hours The group began to realise that the previous days sessions which had been useful rather than productive had been a vital part of experiencing the learning process. By learning more about each other as individuals we were able to form joint assumptions, norms of behaviour and a system of group values to which we all subscribed. We also determined that the leadership of groups requires that the leader knows, and understands the individuals who comprise the group they are leading.

The previous days discussion about who would lead the group had been shelved because there was not an obvious leader and it was more important to work as a leaderless work group, i.e. task orientated. Following the learning process it was, in theory now possible that any member of the group could be the leader, in practice, however the dyad had determined who the leader would be during the previous days sessions, when it was not strategically the right time to force the issue.

During the first session, Dorota constructed a model of the two basic forms of leadership:

Democratic
or
Oppressive

Alexandra used the German word, bundle (to collect sticks), from which Ingor was able to define leadership as:

A consideration of the individual when exercising leadership.

This implies having enough knowledge and information about individuals in order to consider their needs and aspirations. We now felt that we had made progress with our task, and in the formation of our group, we had been able to transcend the artificial barriers of nationality and language by bundling our own interests, devised a model of leadership, and determined that the principles of leadership were the same regardless of the size of the group.

We had two problems left to solve, who would be our leader, and how could we present our findings to the large plenary session, which were chaotic, and in which the other delegates tended to disrupt. We decided to take a quick lunch and return to our room one and a half hours early to finalise the leadership question and plan our presentation, we would also be free of our consultant, even though Ann Barry was probably the best consultant we could have had.

Almost the entire one and a half hours was spent in finally deciding who would be the leader, and Alexandra was the one appointed. Of course the two dyad members had had to develop the leadership criteria that only she could fulfil. However it was the correct choice and with our consultant sitting back in with us we began to plan our presentation. Ann Barry tried to assist us and warned us that it would not work (thanks Ann).

After much discussion we decided that one of the functions of leadership was to take responsibility. This is as true for managers within organisations and as it is for leaders in society in general. The chaos of the large sessions led us to believe that if we did not take responsibility for presenting our findings we would not be able to present them, therefore we decided to hi-jack the large session. As a result the only group which formed at Coesfeld 1996, as opposed to the collection of people in other groups, and which formed democratically, decided to use oppressive leadership to present it's findings, this of course was regretful to all the group members.

The tasks of the group were shared out. Alexandra prepared her presentation, Dorota, drew and coloured the group symbol of a dragon based on the Krackow dragon, Frank and Ingor went to investigate and liaise with the other groups, and Ingor took responsibility for gaining everyone's attention when the large session started.

The group entered the conference room early and prepared the stage with five chairs as the other delegates and the consultants filed into the room. After a false start, Ingor was able to take control of the session and introduce Alexandra.

There was so much opposition to the dragons from the other delegates that we spent most of the time defending our oppressive actions. The key moment in Franks opinion was when someone suggested that the conference should take a vote as to whether or not we should be allowed to speak, the rest of the group let this slip past and, has we had already decided to only take ten minutes for our presentation, to allow the other groups ten minutes for their presentations, we left the stage.

The group merged back into the conference as a whole and the session remained as chaotic as all the other large sessions had been.

The reason, or meaning of existence for the Dragons of Coesfeld ended with the presentation to the conference plenary session on Monday evening. However the dragons continued as a group for the remaining five days of the conference which appeared to be a cause of concern for the consultants, and of amazement to many of the other delegates. The dragons always ate breakfast together, it was a ritual and symbol of the groups unity.

Within the following large sessions, the only sessions in which the whole group continued to be present and together there was a natural, instinctive or unconscious bond for the group members. This bond meant that even though there were no formal plans made, the group always supported each other in the large sessions, while the dyad worked together in all sessions with the exception of the role analysis group.

Discussion

Experiencing now, everyday for eight days means experiencing constantly the interactions and interrelationships that take place in a context, and environment in which there is no time to make secondary or rational adjustments. Experiencing now in this context means making instant primary adjustments. These adjustments are made using the individuals emotion perceptions.

Emotion perceptions involve communication and cognitions which motivate behaviour. They involve feeling into the emotional life of other individuals in order to create a shared emotion life and reality of and for the group.

Emotion works to protect and project individual and group reality and creates a positive or negative energy which the group can use, or be overwhelmed by. The experience of the emotional life of the Dragons of Coesfeld indicates that Bions concept of valency, and the protomental system are compatible with the concept of emotion as a two-tier system of perception, cognition and communication which motivates behaviour. Finally the concept of Coesfeld as a spiritual or intellectual experience is a myth developed by the consultants, although extreme actions and behaviour are experienced at Coesfeld, this is normal. It is only the reaction to extreme stimulation within an extreme context. The myth arises because the way in which emotion works was not fully understood.

References

Argyle, M. (1972), *The Psychology of Interpersonal Behaviour*, Pelican, Harmondsworth.

Bion, W.R. (1996), *Experiences in Groups*, Routledge, London.

Bowles, M.L (1991), *The Organisation Shadow*, Organisational Studies, Vol 23/3 p387.

Czamiaska-Joerges, B. (1993), IER Working Paper Series, *Copy Rights and References*, Lund University, Sweden.

Freud, S. (1966), reprint, *The Psychopathology of Everyday Life*, Ernest Benn, London.

Gagliardi, P. (1990), *Symbols and Artefacts: Views of the Corporate Landscape*, De Gruyter, NY.

Glinka, B. and Lukaszewicz, J. (1996), *The Priests and the Swallow*, paper for the Symbols of Oppression Conference, 27 and 28 March, Bolton Business School.

Goffman, E. (1971), *Asylums*, Pelican, Harmondsworth.

Hochschild, A.R. (1983), *The Managed Heart*, University of California Press, London.

Jung, C.J. (1923), *Psychological Types*, Kegan P, Trench and Trubner & Co Ltd, London.

Jung, C.J. (1977), *The Collected Works*, vol 18, Routledge Kegan P, London.

Katz, J. (1980), 'Discrepancy Arousal and Labelling: Towards a Psychological Theory of Emotion', *Social Enquiry*, vol 50, pp.147/156.

Laing, R.D. (1969), *The Self and Others*, Pelican, Harmondsworth.

Letiche, J. and Vans Mens, L. (1996), *Managing by Oppressiveness*, a paper for the Symbols of Oppression Conference, 27 and 28 March, Bolton Business School.

Llein, M. (1990), reprint, *Melanie Klein Today*, Vol 2, Editor Tucket, D. Tavistock, Routledge, London.

McDougall, W. (1946), *An Introduction to Social Psychology*, 28 Ed, Methuen and Co Ltd, London.

Rokeach, M. (1960), *The Open and Closed Mind*, Basic Books Inc, NY.

Rorty, A.0. (1980), *The Rationality of Emotions*, Berkeley, University of California Press.

Sprott, W.J.H. (1977), *Human Groups*, Penguin, Harmondsworth.

Walter, W.G. (1968), *The Living Brain*, Pelican, Harmondsworth.

10 Use of task groups and teams for management of human resources

A. R. Analouei

Introduction

The terms 'individual', 'group' and 'team' are frequently used, especially in so far as the management of human resources in work organisations are concerned (Smith et. al., 1987). The advocates of the traditional theories and values systems place an inordinate amount of emphasis on the utilisation of individuals at work. The modern management theorists and practitioners, in contrast, perceive the groups and teams as essential building blocks of today's organisations (Mullins, 1994). Nowadays, it is believed that paying attention to group dynamics, the needs and motivation of task groups at work and investment in 'team building' will make a significant contribution to the achievement of greater effectiveness and efficiency at work. Organisations therefore, treat and use people as resources in order to get the job done (Tuckman, 1991).

While the importance of groups and teams can be equally emphasised in both the public and private sectors, arguably it is in the private sector in which the significance of investment in people and their development in the form of training, with regard to group and team building, has been better realised. It is suggested that the concept of group and team gains a greater importance in organisations or enterprises which rely heavily on experts and specialists whose cumulative effort is directed towards 'problem solving', and/or implementation of projects. Often, organisations involved in process innovation, intervention (change agents) and maintenance of change in other institutions and enterprises, such as consultancies, tend to perceive the importance of and the use of task groups/teams in their structure, not only for carrying out the task but also in order to remain competitive (Shien, 1969).

Moreover, consulting organisations ought to benefit from a structure which can offer maximum flexibility and potential in order to be able to provide high quality output to their clients at short notice. The responsibility for bringing about change in the clients organisation, added to the day to day unpredictability and competition faced and the client's expectation for a prompt, efficient and high quality service, all become sources of pressure which can be felt at all levels, management or otherwise This makes the emergence of conflict and tension inevitable and if this conflict is not properly and effectively managed and dealt with it could result in inferior services, let alone a lower quality of the relationships at work (Handy, 1976; Kakabadse et. al., 1987). The use of task groups and teams incorporated into the structure of the organisation can considerably minimise the tension and conflict experienced. Needless to say, this will undoubtedly result in increased performance on the part of the individuals involved (Belbin, 1981).

In this chapter the author[1] will first consider some of the concepts and theories associated with groups and teams in particular in relation to their dynamics and development in the workplace. Then, it will be illustrated, how systematic analysis of the organisation structure and the introduction of tailor-made work groups and team formations at work will result in the provision of a sound and efficient service to the client, improved relationships at work and hence greater success for the organisation as the whole (Pascale and Athos, 1986). Whilst attention will be paid to the ways of developing teams at work, it will be contended that although the task of changing the traditional work patterns into task groups and teams operation is initially difficult, sustainability of those changes then requires the attention, support and motivation of the top management of the organisation (Kakabadse et. al., 1987).

The case of a major US consultancy organisation which has been active at both national and international levels, and in which the author has recently introduced a task group structure, will be discussed. The results and implications which this planned change has had for the management of the human resources, and the effectiveness and efficiency of the organisation will be discussed in some detail and relevant conclusions will be reached.

What is a group?

The terms 'group' and 'team' have been frequently and extensively used, often in relation to work organisations. It has been suggested that 'work' is a group based activity and if the organisation is to function effectively it requires teamwork. The working of the group and the influence which they exert over their membership is an essential feature of human behaviour and of organisational performance (Mullins, 1993, p.168). Groups are evidently used for a variety of purposes and it is not unusual to see that members sometimes attempt to satisfy their individual needs through their groups (Kakabadse et. al., 1987). However, despite this wide usage of the term, often inadequate attempts are made to define and understand what is actually meant by these terms. This is particularly symptomatic of practitioners in industry and professional consultants, who utilise terms and labels, often in their daily dialogue with colleagues and clients, but find it difficult to differentiate between them. Especially, in the context of changing work relationships.

Examination of the literature reveals that some theorists tend to place stress on the individuals motivation for the 'formation' of a group, while others attempt to define groups as that which is perceived by its constituent members. There are also others who believe that the formation and development of group roles and norms as a 'consequence' of group processes is of greater importance (Smith et. al., 1987). It will be argued that not only is all of the above relevant to the ways a dynamic and fast moving consulting organisation functions, but that in industry too managers and professionals can use the same principles to manage and utilise their human resources in a more satisfactory and efficient way.

Those in favour of interaction amongst the members tend to adopt the definition of group which goes on to suggest, 'a group is defined as two or more persons who interact with one another so that each person influences and is influenced by each other' (Shaw, 1971; Argyles, 1989; Grayson, 1990). The two way process of interaction and influence is important. In so far as 'task' is concerned, a group can be defined as either 'a set of persons amongst whom there exists a definable or observable set of relations (Davis, 1969) or more importantly as, 'a set of mutually interdependent behavioural systems that not only affect each other, but respond to exterior influences as well' (Cartwright and Zander, 1968).

Types of group

A distinction however ought to be made between 'formal' and 'informal' groups. In that, although the 'processes' and dynamics are similar, in both types the 'context' will be rather different. The latter category seems to usually and naturally take form in all organisations and it has been argued that their formation has often been a response, either consciously or unconsciously, to certain felt 'social needs' and their satisfaction (Schultz, 1958; Berne, 1967; Kogan, 1975). The existence of 'informal groups' is often attributed to chance or personal preference. The informal network of relationships is, by and large, a healthy and necessary activity in all organisations, simply because it enables managers and employees to collect information, which is sometimes necessary for their work, via means of interpersonal interactions. However, as will be stressed later, when informal groupings or a collection of individuals are used to 'get the job done' management can exert little or no control over their relationships. In such cases, the accountability and interdependency necessary in order to ensure that the task is carried out satisfactorily, will be none existent and therefore the satisfactory achievement of the organisational objectives cannot be guaranteed (Cummings, 1985).

Formal groups, which as will be shown, can be developed into responsible and effective teams, are distinguishable from 'informal' ones by their definable 'content', which relates them and their efforts to the organisation, its objectives and goals. In other words, the formal group is specifically and purposefully created to carry out a function (task). The processes involved in terms of interactions and interpersonal relationships are vital for its success, but it is the task which is the main reason for its formation and therefore, it is the task which can define the roles and contribution expected of the members. To adopt Schien's (1986) definition, 'both groups, whether formal or informal, are made up of a number of people who (1) interact with one another; (2) are psychologically aware of one another; and (3) perceive themselves as a group' (p.145).

For the purpose of our discussion, it will be emphasised that work related groups ought to be formed purposely and intentionally and that it is the task of the manager or group leader to ensure that the group members perceive themselves as a group or a team (Analoui, 1993). Other distinctions have also been made to extend the classification into 'primary groups' and 'secondary groups' (Rackham et. al., 1967). In the context of a consultancy group or organisation, primary groups refers to a small number of people (in this case, experts) who perform a common task and have regular personal interaction with each other. As will be demonstrated, the group used for structuring the 'Transitional Service' (TS) at InfoPro Incorporated, the case study, was identifiable by its label partly because of the emphasis on 'common task'. TA was meant to operate as a main group but it lacked structure, cohesion and other aspects identifiable by 'Primarily Task Groups'. Also, there is the 'secondary group' at InfoPro which, unlike the primary group' consists of a larger number of people who do not have the opportunity to have much personal interaction with one another. In a sense the organisation as a whole is a secondary group to which all consultants have membership, but with varying degrees of intensity of interaction.

Problems confronted by work groups

Smith et. al., (1987) aptly summarises the difficulties that work groups face, as twofold.

- To achieve the 'task' for which it has been set up.
- To 'maintain' itself as a cohesive unit so that its members feel part of a team.

It has also been suggested that the above processes are separate and are mutually antagonistic. When a group is working on task activities, it is creating problems for itself by remaining a team (Bales, 1951). Some believe that group interaction is basically of three types; 'task', 'maintenance' and' self-orientated' behaviours (Argyle, 1979). Moreover, it is argued that it is the third behaviour that may create tension and conflict, if the first function is not given adequate attention, direction and leadership.

For the purpose of the present discussion it would be more meaningful if the task group (team) can be perceived in the context of 'what?' it is that the groups sets out to achieve and 'how?' the group members behave in relation to one another. The former relates to the 'task' and the latter describes the 'processes' involved (see Figure 10.1).

Figure 10.1 has major implications for the development, as well as the management of the task groups. These will be referred to in more detail when the change of structure, from that which was formerly known as 'Transitional Services' to the new 'Team Management', is discussed. It is important however, to note that not only the organisations objectives, goals, strategies and established work processes determine the need for and emergence of groups and teams, it is often the realisation or vision of one or all members of the top management or others and the availability of expert resources (in this case human resources developer) which makes the vision become reality. Therefore, a consultancy organisation whose main goal is providing services may carry within itself a potential change agent who may direct the attention of top management and the organisations resources towards a more effective and efficient way of organising itself. It is of great importance to bear in mind that the formation of task group and team structure is only part of the overall solution and that its management ought to provide a shield of support around the initiator or the change agent to ensure the survivability and maintenance of the new system, if it is to remain viable and functional on a steady uphill trend (Kakabadse, 1983; Analoui, 1997).

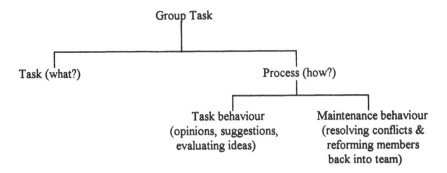

Figure 10.1 A taxonomy of group activities

Source: Smith et. al., (1987) 'Introducing Organisational Behaviour', p.139.

The nature of the task to be carried out as an organisation, in this case a major consultancy organisation in the field of Information Technology with national (US) and international clients in both developed and developing countries, determines the purpose for which the task groups are used. Handy (1976) summaries the purpose for using groups as follows;

1. For the distribution of work, to bring together a set of skills, talents and responsibilities and allocate them their particular duties.
2. For management and control of the work.
3. For problem solving and decision taking.
4. For the processing of information.
5. For collecting ideas and information.
6. For testing and verifying decisions.
7. For co-ordinating and liaison.
8. For generally increased commitment and involvement.

9. For negotiation and conflict resolution.
10. For inquest and inquiry into the past.

At InfoPro, the author's decision to use a task group and team structure was based on more than one of the above factors. For example, the distribution of the consultants, the effective use of their skills and expertise, allocation of work and most importantly, the presence of 'control' and 'accountability' were considered important. As will be explained, the former structure with a pool of (TS) consultants available to the other Directorates of the organisation had proved to be dysfunctional since it increased tension, conflict and generally lowered the performance and quality of the services rendered. The organisation also assumed the problem solving role as well as the collection of ideas and information. But for the author, aside from the obvious reasons, it was the general increase in commitment, negotiation and conflict resolution and more importantly, co-ordination and liaison which formed the main reasons for adopting the group or team formation.

Development of a group to a team

All groups go through various stages of development and a work team's effectiveness is also a product of how the team has managed to cope with the problems it faces in each of its developmental stages (Handy, 1985; Allcorn, 1989). Studies have shown that team development is primarily concerned with the interactions between individual members to form a cohesive integrated unit. It is suggested that developing into an integrated and self supporting team will involve the following broad strategies (Belbin, 1987; Cummings, 1985).

- Assisting the team members to become acquainted.
- Helping members to offer feed back. Helping members to establish criteria.
- Encouraging members to take part in the running, developing and maintenance of the relationships amongst its members.

The team's membership is not normally voluntarily. The work relationships are usually well defined and established.

Nowadays, most middle-sized and large firms, projects and almost all institutions, are run by small management teams. Each member holding a position of responsibility and his or her efforts contributes to the effectiveness of the team (Smith et. al., 1987; Analoui, 1994).

A shift in power and authority away from one individual and towards a team, amongst many things, is thought to protect the organisation against corruption and the problem of indispensability. Team management has become the stable alternative, a means of viewing a business and/or a project effective so long as the right combination of people can be found.

Effective team development

It is true that a perfect team requires the combination of right individuals with a selection of desired abilities and characteristics. However, it is unrealistic to expect that, by simply placing a number of skilled professional individuals in a group should be expected to perform as a team (Kakabadse et. al., 1987). For teams to perform effectively it requires time: time for team members to be acquainted with each other, to assess each other's strengths and weaknesses and to reflect whether they can identify with the values, beliefs, attitudes and general style of their colleagues, individuals or the whole group.

One of the areas of research critical to both understanding and developing effective teams is how a disparate group develops into an effective working team. Team Development Wheel as a means of training managers to perform as team members. It was concluded that teams experience four distinct stages in their development from a group of individuals to a more cohesive unit.

These are:

> Forming
> Storming
> Norming
> Performing

Forming

At this stage the individual members need to become acquainted and to know more about one another. Naturally they are somewhat inhibited. Their behavioural patter is likely to be 'polite' probably 'impersonal', 'guarded' in disclosing personal or work orientated information or even offering an opinion. In short they test each others personalities, professional capabilities and the degree of commitment to the group and tasks in hand, and more importantly how they should be carried out.

Storming

Once the group members have gained confidence and started working on the tasks in hand, a certain amount of 'infighting' is likely to occur. Leadership of the group is the one which is most likely to induce infighting amongst the members. The competition for leadership often leads to a split between the members and the conflict emerges. Differences in opinion leads to taking sides and as a result some team members may opt out. The overall feeling is that of 'feeling demotivation' and the 'feeling of being stuck'.

Norming

How long the storming stage takes is, by and large, dependent upon the quality of the group's leadership and whether or not the group members have decided to get on with the tasks in hand. Usually by doing the tasks allocated to the group and meeting the targets set. The norms of behaviour and professional practice begin to be established. The interpersonal barriers begin to disappear though the infighting may still occur from time to time. Many groups during their development stage, do not go beyond stage three and regress back to the previous stage. This is a common characteristic of groups which cannot agree on leadership or have not established their group norms and so on. Such groups need to be identified and assisted so that they can break out of this vicious circle.

Performing

Often, the group cannot break away from regressing back to previous stages and needs help from its leader. A sympathetic leader with interpersonal skills, counselling and listening skills, who can use those skills to help members identify with a mission or purpose. A skilled leader realises that shaping a meaningful identity for the group is the most likely to carry it into stage four.

Once in stage four, the group become more cohesive. Group members are more supportive of each other's differences. A greater professional closeness begins to emerge. As a result of utilising each other's strengths and talents to a greater degree, the team becomes more resourceful and flexible in its approach to performing as a genuine team.

It must be noted that to untrained individual, the performance of newly formed team is acceptable simply because it is above average. However, the true potential of the team can only be realised when, and only when, the team has managed to survive 'storming' and 'norming' and finally reaches the 'performing' stage. At InfoPro the team development has already indicated that those who do not fit into the new team work structure and cannot cope with its responsibilities and roles and true accountability have to leave: a response which is perfectly understandable in an organisation at the cutting edge of information technology and consultancy activity.

Having said that, more is needed in order to establish or 'refreeze' the formed relationships at work. The support of the top management to the team leader usually translates to improved quality of work and task related efforts on the part of the team members (Smith et. al., 1987; Shaw, 1976).

The supported leader will be able to:

- Encourage professional and team growth development.
- Ensure team adopts a positive attitude towards the task in hand.
- There ought to be one accountability line within team.
- Keep the team as small as possible.
- Pay attention the differing demands of the team members; and
- Ensure that team operates on a disciplining basis, in an interdisciplinary style, and co-operates with other parts of the organisation and outside agencies.

Effective establishment of task groups (teams): A case study

InfoPro Incorporated (IP) is a recognised leader in the provision of Information Technology (IT) services to the US Government and commercial enterprises nation wide. It also provides services to international clients. For example, in Eastern European countries such as Romania. It has the capacity to compete on a global level. The organisation specialises in delivering integrated business solutions that maximise the return on technology investment. On the whole, IP concentrates on three primary areas - Business Transition, Network Support and Software Support.

The specialist services offered place the organisation in a unique but highly competitive market. It deals with change in a strategic and planned form as well as offering support and maintenance to both the public and private sectors for maintenance up keep of the installed systems.

The structure of the organisation is typically hierarchical, but designed in a flat form to be responsive to the changes in the market and to meet the ever changing demands of their clients and the changes in the world of IT as the whole. The strategic apex comprises of three executives who form the

Executive Committee. Hitherto the organisation was a two-tier structure, partly hierarchical and partly unstructured. A number of Program Managers whom were responsible for major 'contracts' each and occupied the second line of authority, each 'Program Manager' resourced with 50 or more individuals, some specialists and others who are responsible for administrative duties. For example, the 'Program Manager' for PBS was responsible for the Public Building Services Program. This included the management of the information systems of the Federal Building's computers and software system.

The Program Managers, Group Managers, Task Leaders and Developers held varying degrees of responsibility within the hierarchical structure of the organisation respectively. For example, the Program Manager receives the advice, funding and resources necessary to deal with a contract, assumes the role of the 'customer advocate' and ensures the contact with the client. Group Managers provide the necessary advice functions, including programme writing. The PBS Program, for example, comprised of 60 or more sub-projects. These projects are divided between the group managers who have access to permanent (few staff) resources who are under their control and, when required, could access resources from another part of the organisation, namely the 'Transition Services'. It is the structure of this part of the organisation, which holds a number of the specialised resources, that has major implications for the way InfoPro has operated to date.

Transition services (TR) and the need for change

Alongside the hierarchically structured part of the organisation which dealt with the major contracts, there was also a need for the provision of resources to the Group Managers - on a need to have basis. Traditionally the director of TS preferred to provide a pool of services which in fact formed a collection of structurally unrelated staff (specialists) who were on loan to other parts of the organisation as resources. This unstructured pool of resources meant that the director in charge was exercising complete control over individuals but offered little in return in terms of management of resources available. This led to the company experiencing various difficulties regarding the efficient use of its resources (experts), and tensions and conflict amongst the staff and departments across the company as the whole.

The Program Managers, for example, avoided using the internal resources and sometimes resorted to 'buying in' from outside organisations, a costly process which is both disruptive and damaging to the integrity of the organisation. Moreover, often when the resources from the TR's 'pool' were loaned to other Program Managers, they tended to leave the pool permanently, a condition referred to internally as the 'Black Hole Effect'. The uncertainty experienced by the specialist members of the pool, the lack of a coherent structure or specific lines of accountability meant that the Director of the TS could not manage the resources in a meaningful way, consequently allowing the situation of low morale to persist which forced the top management to respond to the deteriorating situation in so far as TS was concerned.

It is important to note, that the resources in the form of a pool should not be mistaken with what is known as Infrastructure which is comprised of computer services, pay role and administrative personnel, whose function is to offer services and support internally to all levels of the organisation. The TS on the other hand, was meant to deal with the demands of the other parts of the organisation by providing them with enough resources to adequately manage the projects in hand. The Executive Committee who became aware of the chaotic nature of the relationships within the TS, attempted to remedy the situation in the conventional way. It was therefore assumed that what was required was in fact another line of management between the Head of TS and the top management.

Individual 'B', attempted to resolve the problem by effectively dismantling the TS. He therefore announced that 'there ought not to be a TS, nor even a core of staff at all'. Hence the pool of staff should be integrated into the staff of directors who managed major programs such as the PBS. This meant that the organisation structure would have to become more bureaucratic hence loosing the flexibility which it was meant to offer. This unsatisfactory solution added further to the chaos and forced the Top Executive Committee to intervene. The author was approached to offer practical solutions. The attempts at this stage were not directed at only solving the original problem but first and foremost to remedy the problems which had been created as a result of the improper restructuring.

After an initial examination of the organisation goals, objectives and task processes involved, as well as auditing the human resources available - albeit informally - the author assumed the role of consultant (with support from the top executives) and began to act as an 'internal change agent'. It was felt that a form of structure was needed which would be both cohesive and flexible and at the same time not so loosely defined as to allow members of the 'services' to escape responsibility either intentionally or unintentionally. In other words, the intention was to place the emphasis on 'task', as opposed to political influence, which had been enjoyed by a few role players before.

The solution offered in fact incorporated a mix of task groups and team structure which, unlike similar structures in the industry, maintained its cohesion by providing a micro 'task culture' in which the informality and flexibility were maximised, but simultaneously the individuals felt and perceived their position in the 'team' structure to comprise of well defined roles.

Instead of a pool of resources, now the proposed structure comprised of Lead (Project Manager) and team members, who were responsible for projects (4), and were comprised of 8 direct supervisors and 20 resources. The creation of teams and sub-groups for teams, who were highly task-related, provided stability and increased morale and accountability. It also provided a basis for auditing the resources which were available internally.

The diagram which explains the work relationships and accountability lines, to the Lead, and soon became known as the Bubble Diagram (Figure 10.2), a term given to the roles provided in the new structure. However, in order to ensure the flexibility required and the availability of resources, the new structure had to take advantage of 'flexible role responsibility'. Members of the 'bubble' are also involved in the provision of services to other parts of the organisation and at the same time are responsible for their allocated responsibilities and tasks.

The sensitivity of the structure necessitated the use of a less rigid superstructure which should allow the Lead to take charge of the team structure (resources) and to work directly with the executives as well as the directors who required services and resources from the teams to meet the demands of the major programs. This meant that the position of middle management seemed not only unnecessary and but arguably also a barrier between the team leader (Project Manager) responsible for getting the job done and the Executive Management who could offer support and direction to 'Services' and other directorates, as the whole.

Development and maintenance

As indicated earlier, the formation of groups and teams provide a basis for the effective management of resources and efficient operation of the consultancy as a whole. However, it requires the following:

- periodic assessment of the team members to ensure their suitability (task or nature) within the team structure;
- planned team building training which can be change, cohesion and commitment on the part of the individuals; and most important of all

Bubble Diagram

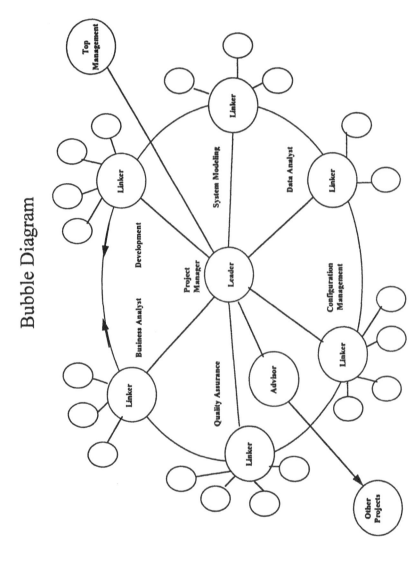

Figure 10.2   Distribution of human resources amongst the task-groups

154

- support from the executives (Top Management) for the Lead, in terms of availability of resources, authority, recognition and direct communication so that the Lead can pay adequate attention to both the task-related aspects as well as the maintenance processes of the team which are necessary for its healthy operations.

The support of the executives, amongst other things, ensures that cognitive dissonance, naturally created amongst other directors (the grass is greener on the other side) can be effectively neutralised. Top Management's support will now take on both informative and protective forms.

Since the formation of the new team structure, staff morale has risen considerably with an immediate effect on the performance and output of the individual experts involved. It has also provided a structure for the Top Management to effectively assess and audit the resources which they have at their disposal within the organisation. In addition to the above, top management do not feel that they have to assume the time consuming role of the 'fire fighters' and permanent 'disturbance handlers', hence optimising the resources for strategic planning for the improved future role of the organisation in the demanding world of Information Technology.

Conclusion

Undoubtedly, there is a complex, yet direct, relationship between the form and structure of the human resources in an organisation and the philosophy of the management in charge of the organisation. In fact managerial philosophy in operation reflects the intent and degree of the commitment shown in terms of how the resources are organised, managed and their contribution utilised towards the achievement of the organisations objectives. The use of task groups and teams, as shown earlier, apart from maximising the invested returns in staff time and resources, tends to have a 'self-regulating' as well as motivating effect. It also provides a platform for optimising the use of resources as well as enabling the management to have better control over the 'processes' involved in the organisation including 'task', 'responsibility', 'accountability' and most importantly receiving accurate feedback from the clients of organisation.

What, however, is of the utmost importance is to recognise that group and team structures, unlike bureaucratic set ups, require formal support from the top management of the organisation. Support received from the top management provides adequate power leverage for the team manager to elevate the standard of performance amongst team members and to create a climate of co-operation and dedication to task so that the ideals, visions and strategic plan of the top management are effectively realised. Of course, the dynamic processes involved in the formation and development of the task groups and teams, necessitates the use of on going training and motivation to ensure a high level of performance and standards.

Note

1. The author wishes to thank the Executive Committee for their assistance throughout the process, in particular, Mr. Ali Saadat for his invaluable support, contribution and comments. However, it must be noted that the views and opinions expressed in this chapter do not reflect InfoPro's official policies or practices, but are those of the author alone.

References

Allcorn, S. (1989), Understanding Groups at Work', *Personnel*, Vol.66, no.8 August, pp.28-36.

Analoui, F. (1993), 'Management Skills' Chapter Five in *Management of Projects within Developing Countries*, edited by Cusworth, J; Frank, T; Longman Scientific and Technical, London.

Analoui, F. (1994) (ed.), *Realities of Management Development Projects*, Avebury, Aldershot.

Analoui, F (1997), *Senior Managers and Their Effectiveness*, Avebury, Aldershot.

Argyris, M. (1989), *Social Psychology of Work*, Second Edition, Penguin.

Bales, R. F. (1951), *Interaction Processes Analysis: A method for the study of small groups*, Addison-Wesley, Reading, Mass.

Belbin, R. D. (1981), *Management of Teams: why they succeed or fail*, Heinemann, USA.

Berne, E. (1967), *Games People Play*, Grove Press.

Cartwright, P. Zander, A. (1968), *Group Dynamics: research and theory*, Third Edition, Harper and Row.

Cummings, T. G. (1985), *Designing Effective Work Groups*, Penguin, London.

Davids, K. (1977), *Human Behaviour at Work*, Fifth Edition, McGraw-Hill, p.183.

Grayson, D. (1990), 'Self-regulating Work groups; An aspect of organisational change' ACAS, Work Research Unit, Occasional Paper, no.146, HMSO, July.

Handy, C. B. (1985), *Understanding Organisation*, Third Edition, Penguin.

Kakabadse, A. (1983), *Politics of Management*, Gower, UK.

Kakabadse, A; Ludlow, R; Vinnicombe, S. (1987), *Working in Organisations*, Gower, UK.

Kogan, N. (1975), *Interpersonal Process Recall: A method of influencing human interaction*, Ann Arbor, Michigan State University Press.

Mullins, L.J. (1993), *Management and Organisational Behaviour*, Third Edition, Pitman, Publishing.

Pascal, R. Athos, A. (1986), *The Art of Japanese Management*, Sidgwick & Jackson, London.

Rackman, N. Hong, P. Colbert, M. (1967), *Developing Interaction Skills*, Wellons Publishing, Northampton.

Schien, E. H. (1988), *Organisational Psychology*, Third Edition, Prentice-Hall, p.145.

Schultz, W.C. (1958), *FIRO: The Three Dimensional Theory of Interpersonal Behaviour*, Holt, Rinehart and Winston.

Shaw, M. E. (1971), *Group Dynamics: The psychology of small group behaviour*, McGraw-Hill, New York.

Smith, M; Beck, J; Cooper, C.L; Cox, C; Ottaway, D; Talbot, R. (1987), *Introductory Organisational Behaviour*, MacMillan Education.

Tuckman, B. W. (1991), *Development Sequences in Small Groups*, Penguin, London.

11 Measuring human development: some improvements on the human development index

Farhad Noorbakhsh

Introduction

For more than four decades the adequacy of gross national product as a measure of the welfare of a society has been questioned. Nevertheless the overemphasis of development programmes and plans on economic growth models has remained almost intact. What has probably been overlooked by some economists and practitioners is that economic growth does not necessarily translate into human welfare, though it may be considered as a major, but not the sole, component of any definition of such a concept.

A group of experts on social policy and planning in 1969 expressed concerns that overemphasis on economic growth neglects and in some cases may even create poverty and be an obstacle to social progress (UN, 1969). Some scholars suspected that '... the economic growth by itself may not solve or even alleviate the problem (of poverty) in any reasonable time period' (Chenery, et. al., 1976, p.1). It has also been suggested that our perception of the concept of development should change by changing the focus from commodities to people (Noorbakhsh, 1976). In an attempt to define the concept of development Seers (1972) regarded it as '... creating the conditions for realisation of human potentiality'.

Such concerns resulted in a search for alternative measures of human welfare (development). Amongst the early attempts we may refer to the 'levels of living index' (Drewnowski, et. al., 1966) and 'development index' (McGranahan, et. al., 1972). Another measure, developed later, excluded the income component altogether. The 'physical quality of life index' (PQLI) had three social components: infant mortality rate, life expectancy and adult literacy (Morris, 1979).[1] Furthermore some scholars argued for a change in the objectives of development programmes and proposed the

159

satisfaction of basic needs as a replacement for purely macroeconomic objectives (Hicks and Streeten, 1979; Streeten, et. al., 1981) thus moving the emphasis towards human objectives.[2]

The most recent attempt in constructing a measure of human development is the annual publication of the Human Development Index (HDI) by the UNDP since 1990. This index has gone through a certain amount of scrutiny in the literature. Some of its criticisms are related to the idea of measuring human development by a conceptually limited composite index, some have regarded it to have limited scope in measuring human development due to the quality and limitation of data (Murray, 1993; Srinivasan, 1994) while some others have considered it to be redundant (McGillivray, 1991). Despite this the HDI has been favoured on the grounds that it shows the inadequacy of other indices such as GNP (Streeten, 1994 and 1995)[3]. It has been preferred to per capita income as the latter neglects the distributional aspects (Desai, 1993) and it has been suggested that it 'captures many aspects of human development' (Haq, 1995, p.54). Generally the constituent indicators of this index are considered to provide a comprehensive package of indices at a very aggregate level (Dasgupta and Weale, 1992).

Some other critics have been concerned with the technical properties of this composite index. A few criticisms have resulted in changes in the structure of the HDI in more recent years (Trabold-Nubler, 1991).

This chapter critically examines the technical aspects of the HDI and its updated versions and makes some recommendations for improving the content and structure of this index. The data from Human Development Report 1994 for 173 countries are used to test the robustness of this modified index and the results are compared to those of the HDI. The new index is then used to delineate, with some justification, different groups of countries at various levels of human development.

The human development index

The HDI is a composite index of four indicators. Its components are to reflect three major dimensions of human development: longevity, knowledge and access to resources. These are to represent three of the essential choices 'for people to lead a long and healthy life, to acquire knowledge and to have access to resources needed for a decent standard of living' (HDR, 1990).

Life expectancy at birth is selected to measure the longevity, knowledge is represented by a measure of educational achievement based on a weighted sum of adult literacy rate and mean years of schooling with access to resources being measured by an adjusted real purchasing power parity GDP per capita.

It is generally accepted that HDI does not properly represent the concept of human development (HDR, 1993), where the latter goes beyond the proposed dimensions of the former and can not be fully caught in 'any index or set of indicators' (Streeten, 1994, p.235). It is, therefore, at best a summary index.

The technical aspects of HDI for the purpose of our discussion may be referred to as those related to the constituents of the HDI and those related to the construction of the index itself.

Access to resources and knowledge

Income indicator Access to the resources dimension was originally represented by the real per capita income, purchasing power parity in dollar (PPP$), of countries adjusted with reference to the average of poverty-line income in several developed countries (y^*). In the 1994 report this threshold value was replaced by the current average global value of real GDP per capita in PPP$.

In the 1990 report income above y^* had no contribution to the HDI as a cap at the poverty line was introduced for countries with income higher than y^*. In effect incomes for countries above the poverty line were reduced to the poverty-line income. Moreover, the logarithm of income was used for calculating the HDI. The combination of introducing a cap and taking the logarithm of income was to reflect, rather sharply, the diminishing marginal contribution of income to the human development (HDR, 1991).

Practically this resulted in the HDI having three components for those countries with income equal or below y^* while it had only two components (plus a constant) for countries with an income above the threshold as the value of the income component for the latter group of countries remained the same.

Subsequent reports accepted that income above y^* will have some effect on the HDI. This modification was to take into consideration the wider 'people's choice' rendered through higher income. This was reflected by using the Atkinson formulation for the utility of income $W(y)$:

$$W(y) = (\frac{1}{1-\varepsilon})y^{1-\varepsilon} \tag{1}$$

Parameter ε is to measure the extent of diminishing returns and reflects the deviation of the elasticity of the utility of income with respect to income from unity. Given the Atkinson formula the marginal utility of income is: $dW(y)/dy = y^{-\varepsilon}$ which in turn implies that the elasticity of the utility of income with respect to income would be $(1-\varepsilon)$. As $\varepsilon \to 0$, fractions of income above poverty level will have a more significant effect and for $\varepsilon = 0$ the dollar for dollar effect is reflected fully. It should also be noted that the notion of diminishing returns applies to moving from one selected interval to the next.

Different values were assigned to ε reflecting the extent of the diminishing returns associated with higher levels of income. For income up to the poverty-line income ε was set to zero resulting in no diminish in returns. Income above y^* was to be divided into selected intervals. In general the suggested intervals for income y falling in the range of $ay^* \le y \le (a+\delta)y^*$ may be determined by the prescribed values for parameters a and δ. The UNDP put $\delta = 1$ and = prescribed a=1 and a=2 ..., reflecting one fold and two fold ..., additional y^* income. This corresponded with a general form of $\varepsilon = a/(a+1)$ resulting in $\varepsilon = 1/2$ and $\varepsilon = 2/3$ ... respectively. These determined the diminishing returns of income over the selected ranges. [4]

Treating fragments of income differently is a sensible proposition, however the question is whether the prescribed range would allow for an adequate consideration of income above the poverty line. In other words would the suggested intervals, determined by the selected value for δ, and the prescribed values for ε sufficiently reflect the extent of differences in people's choice?

Selected intervals seem to reduce the contribution of the multiples of income above y^* drastically. This does not seem to be in line with the proposition that higher income would widen people's choice. For example the per capita income differentials of PPP$16222 between Switzerland and Turkey translates into PPP$422 in 1990 (HDR, 1993). In the context of HDI it means that income differentials between two countries, when one or both countries have an income above y^*, will be suppressed rather harshly.

More importantly it seems that one convenience of the UNDP approach is that the elasticity is derived from the selected width of the intervals. While it is sensible to set different values for ε_i for ordinal i fractions of income above y^* there seems to be little justification for deriving ε_i directly from the selected width of the interval.

With reference to the treatment of the income indicator the 1993 report admits that 'the issue is still under scrutiny'. The report suggests that a logarithmic transformation of this variable is 'a strong challenge to the current approach' (HDR, 1993, p.107). It seems that such a transformation in fact would condense the differentials even more harshly than the adopted approach while the emphasis should be in the opposite direction.

In the 1994 HDI technically this component remained the same except that the threshold value, y^*, was determined by the global average value of real GDP per capita in PPP\$ rather than the average of the poverty level of industrial countries, however, the report provides little support for such a preference. Although this results in an increase in the value of y^* it is of little significance to those countries with middle/high income levels. For example, the per capita income differentials of PPP\$16940 between Switzerland and Turkey in 1994 report now translates into PPP\$530. Furthermore, the upper threshold income of PPP\$40000 translates to PPP\$5385 while an income of PPP\$22130 (Unites States) translates to PPP\$5371 and an income of PPP\$7680 (Greece) converts to PPP\$5221. The average income of PPP\$5120 and below would remain the same.

Educational attainment Knowledge is represented by a measure of educational achievement based on a weighted sum of adult literacy rate and mean years of schooling. That is:

E = a_1 Literacy + a_2 Mean Years of schooling

The arbitrarily selected weights are: $a_1 = 2/3$ and $a_2 = 1/3$. In recent years (HDR 1992 to HDR 1994) indices of these indicators were employed in order to avoid the possibility of different scales affecting the weights unintentionally.[5] This results in:

$$E = a_1 LI + a_2 MI \hspace{4cm} (2)$$

where LI and MI are the indices of the respective stock variables (highest value = 100).

There can be little doubt that the principle of diminishing returns also applies to educational attainments. To put it in a positive context, the early 'units' of educational attainments to a country should be of much higher value than the last ones. In the context of policy making in a country with 30 per cent adult literacy, improvements in literacy are of far greater value than the same for a country with 90 per cent adult literacy.

It may be argued that an appropriate functional form which would capture such diminishing returns is the exponential function, e^x with a specific range of values for x. The range of $-1 < x < 0$ associated with different ranges of adult literacy and combined enrolment ratio indicators were considered to

163

be acceptable for our purpose. The proposed ranges for both indicators, with the associated prescribed values for x are presented in Table 11.1.

Table 11.1
Suggested ranges for adult literacy and mean years of schooling

Adult literacy range (AL) %	Mean years of schooling (MS)	x	e^x
$0 < AL \leq 40$	$0 < MS \leq 7$	0	1.000
$40 < AL \leq 50$	$7 < MS \leq 8$	-0.1	0.905
$50 < AL \leq 60$	$8 < MS \leq 9$	-0.2	0.819
$60 < AL \leq 70$	$9 < MS \leq 10$	-0.3	0.741
$70 < AL \leq 80$	$10 < MS \leq 11$	-0.4	0.670
$80 < AL \leq 90$	$11 < MS \leq 12$	-0.5	0.606
$90 < AL \leq 100$	$12 < MS \leq 13$	-0.6	0.549

For example, the adult literacy (AL) of 81.9 per cent for Turkey in the HDR 1994 will now be valued as follows:

$$AL = 40+9.05+8.19+7.41+6.70+1.15 = 72.5\%$$

The principle point which needs reiterating is that inevitably in the process of constructing HDI we have to make some subjective decisions, it would be better if we can make the subjectivity of such decisions explicit and improve them technically. We regard the suggested approach technically better than that adopted by the UNDP.

The use of similar ranges for both indicators are further justified on the grounds of observing close similarities between the ranges of variations in both series.

The structure of HDI

Up to the 1993 report the HDI was defined as the deviation of the average of three indices from unity. More specifically for country i:

$$HDI_i = 1 - \frac{1}{3}\sum_{j=1}^{3} D_{ij} \tag{3}$$

where D_{ij} is the human deprivation index in country i with respect to each of the three components of the index. This index for country i and component j was calculated as the ratio of the distance between the maximum value of the countries and the value for the ith country to the difference between maximum and minimum values observed over all countries. That is for country i:

$$D_{ij} = \frac{MaxX_j - X_{ij}}{MaxX_j - MinX_j} \quad , \text{ for } j=1,2,3. \tag{4}$$

This would result in HDI values being between 1 and 0; the nearest to 1 the better the HDI. A country with the highest X_{ij} for the jth component would have a deprivation index of zero for that component, and if this is the case for all three components she would have the highest value of 1 for its HDI. Similarly the further away the actual value of X_{ij} from the maximum X_j the nearer the D_{ij} of that component to 1 resulting in HDI tending towards zero.

This dependence of D_{ij} on the distance between the maximum and minimum values raised a few problems. HDR 1994 notes: 'This scaling could produce a frustrating outcome, since a country might improve its performance on life expectancy or educational attainment but see its HDI score fall because the top or bottom countries have done even better - in effect moving the goal posts.' (p.92).

The dependence on the distance between maximum and minimum values is questionable on the grounds that as this distance increases D_{ij} can decrease resulting in an increase in HDI, and vice versa. This means that although a country's level of a specific component of HDI from one year to another may not increase actually, a drop (increase) in Min X_j for that component can result in an improved (worse) HDI for that country. Even if there is a drop in the level of component j for country i the drop in Min X_j may offset this decrease to the extent that it would result in a decrease in D_{ij} resulting in an increase in HDI. In effect it is possible for a country's HDI to change in a direction opposite to the movement of the components of HDI for her, simply because there has been a change in Min X_j. It should be pointed out that we are not suggesting that HDI for a country should not be measured with respect to the values of the components for other countries; what we are saying is that Min X_j may not be the best reference value.

In the 1994 report the HDI has been calculated differently. The index has been directly computed from the following formula:

165

$$HDI_i = \frac{1}{3}\sum_{j=1}^{3} I_{ij}$$ (5)

where for country i:

$$I_{ij} = \frac{X_{ij} - MinF_j}{MaxF_j - MinF_j} \qquad , \text{for } j=1,2,3.$$ (6)

X_{ij} is the actual value of component j for country i. Min F_j and Max F_j are fixed subjectively for four constituent indicators. Life expectancy range is set between 25 to 85 years while that of adult literacy is between zero and 100 percent. The selected extreme values for the mean of schooling years are zero and 15 years (for 1994 HDI) and those of combined enrolment ratio are zero and 100 percent (for 1995 HDI). The minimum and maximum values set for income are PPP$200 and $40000.

The first point is that the extreme values for F_j seem to have been selected rather subjectively with little justification. In fact the only technical change in the construction of index is that of the subjectivity of the selected Min F_j and Max F_j. In other words for the same Min F_j and the same Max F_j it is possible to demonstrate that 1-D_{ij} in the 1993 approach would be equal to the right hand side of equation (6) which was used for the calculation of HDI in 1994 and 1995.

The report argues that these fixed 'normative' values have been selected as the extreme values observed or expected over a long period. It may be argued that the expectations of the value of an indicator over a long period is very likely to be a subjective estimate. Also one may suggest that Min F_j observed over a long period may not be a suitable bench mark for all countries. It may also be said that there are ranges of values for both Min F_j and Max F_j which may be equally acceptable on the same grounds. However, depending on the selected extreme values the values of the computed indices would be different for each component.

For example a change in Min F and Max F for life expectancy from 25 and 85 to 20 and 80 in 1994 HDI would change the value of this component of the index for Gabon by 0.08. Similarly changing Min F for adult literacy from zero to 20 per cent would change the value of this indicator for Gabon from 0.625 to 0.531.

The problem is that as HDI is the average of the sum of three equally weighted indices, it follows that the absolute value of each component will affect the level of HDI. Hence the selected extreme values would affect the value of the index. One may suggest that the effect is only a scale shift which would be the same for all countries. However, as HDI has been used over different time periods for following the progress of different countries and also as it has been used for grouping countries into high, medium and low HDI groups, the scaling effect from one year to another may prove to be significant. Furthermore the scale 'shift' would not be of the same magnitude for all the components of the HDI.

In the light of this the subjectivity of the selected 'yardstick' becomes important as it itself is a linear and is an equally weighted combination of a set of different yardsticks.[6] In other words the absolute value of each component of HDI is sensitive to the choice of these fixed values which are selected somewhat subjectively.

In general re-scaling of data for an indicator to 0-1 range is to some extent arbitrary. In the case of individual components this may be tolerated. However, it can become a problem when the re-scaled components are added to form a composite index.

Furthermore, as the denominator of each component is constant for all countries, in effect the measure is based on the difference between the value of the indicator for the country and a subjectively selected Min F_j. The role of the denominator in equation (6) is in effect that of indexing. This means that with respect to the individual components any range which would result in the denominator being larger than the largest numerator would be technically acceptable. It seems, therefore, that Max F_j would act like an inter-component scaling factor. It is in effect a component weighting factor. Bearing in mind that the HDI is the sum of these scaled components, the scales would have the effect of a set of weights for different components, despite the claim that the components have equal weights in the index. This could result in a change in the ranking order.

To illustrate this point HDI and its components for Ireland and Italy are considered (see Table 11.2).

Table 11.2
Scale effect on the HDI for selected countries

HDI Rank	Country	(1) LE Index	(2) EA Index	(3) GDP Index	(4) HDI	(5)= (1)*1.1	(6)= (2)*0.9	(7) New HDI
21	**Ireland**	0.833	0.860	0.983	**0.892**	0.916	0.774	**0.891**
22	**Italy**	0.865	0.817	0.991	**0.891**	0.952	0.735	**0.893**

Columns (1) to (4) give the index values for life expectancy (LE), educational attainment (EA), GDP per capita and the HDI for four countries as presented in the 1994 HDR. Note that the life expectancy index for Ireland is lower than that of Italy while the position is reversed with respect to the educational attainment index, with little differences in the GDP index. The higher HDI for Ireland ranks her better than Italy.

Now increase the scale of life expectancy component by, for example, 0.1 and decrease the scale of education component by 0.1 with GDP index remaining unchanged (columns 5, 6 and 3 respectively). Column (7) gives the new HDI, the mean of the three indices, for both countries indicating that now Italy is better ranked than Ireland. This demonstrates the sensitivity of HDI to the imposed scale.

In general the simple addition of the components HDI has little justification.[7] To put the argument differently, as the three components of HDI are spread around different means with different variances, the simple averaging of these components for the purpose of building a composite index would be questionable. In addition the means and variances of different components would vary with respect to the selected extreme values for F_j.

A modified human development index (MHDI)

To remove the scale effect and to have the components of HDI spread around the same mean with the same variance, we first standardise the data. The standardised components would then constitute three vectors in a multi-dimensional vector space. Conceptually this makes sense as any index for human development should be defined within the context of all countries. It is important to note that the length of these vectors are equal.

Consider a vector $(X_{ij} - \bar{X}_j)$ containing deviation from mean scores for component j. The length of this vector is given by the square root of the inner product of the vector. That is:

$$\left| X_{ij} - \bar{X}_j \right| = \left[(X_{ij} - \bar{X}_j),(X_{ij} - \bar{X}_j) \right]^{\frac{1}{2}} = \left[\sum_{i=1}^{n}(X_{ij} - \bar{X}_j)^2 \right]^{\frac{1}{2}} \tag{7}$$

From the definition of variance we have:

$$\sigma^2 = \frac{\sum_{i=1}^{n}(X_{ij} - \overline{X}_j)^2}{n} \tag{8}$$

Or

$$\sum_{i=1}^{n}(X_{ij} - \overline{X}_j)^2 = n\sigma^2 \tag{9}$$

Bearing in mind that the variance of a standardised component is equal to 1, from equations (9) and (7)we will have:

$$\left[\sum_{i=1}^{n}(X_{ij} - \overline{X}_j)^2\right]^{\frac{1}{2}} = n^{\frac{1}{2}} = \left|X_{ij} - \overline{X}_j\right| \tag{10}$$

That is, the length of a standardised component vector is equal to the square root of the number of countries which remains the same for all components. Hence the length of the standardised component vectors are equal.

These vectors of equal length can constitute the axes of the space. Countries may then be presented as vectors in this space. In effect in the standardised data matrix, where rows and columns are the countries and components respectively, the vector space consists of the row vectors and the matrix columns are a co-ordinate system for this space. In other words, each country can be mapped as a 3-dimensional vector in the space of the components of HDI. The distance between any two such vectors may then be measured by the length of the so-called distance vector.

Concern can be shown with the distance vector between country i and the country with the maximum standardised score for individual components (the country with the ideal score). Keeping to the same number of components the distance vector d_i for country i will have three components. The length of the distance vector from the best country(ies) for country i is then measured by:

$$d_i = \left[\sum_{j=1}^{3}(Z_{ij} - Z_{oj})^2\right]^{\frac{1}{2}} \tag{11}$$

where Z_{oj} is the standardised score on component j for the ideal country. The lower the d_i the better the position of country i. In order to make this index comparable with the UNDP's HDI the above measure may be reversed and expressed in percentile terms to result in a modified human development index (MHDI), as follows:

$$MHDI_i = 1 - \frac{d_i}{\bar{d} + 2s_d}$$ (12)

where $\bar{d}$ and s_d are the mean and standard deviations of distances for all countries from the ideal country. The second expression on the right hand side of equation (12) reflects the expectation that 95% of cases are between the mean and two standard deviation of the distribution.

Application of MHDI and its comparison with HDI

To test the robustness of the proposed MHDI all the modifications suggested above, those for the individual components as well as those for the construction of the final index, were implemented for computing the MHDI for 173 countries appearing in the HDR 1994 (see Appendix 1).

As shown the countries are ranked according to their MHDI. The ranks of countries by the UNDP's HDI are also provided. It is important to note that the penultimate column of this table provides the HDI rank minus MHDI rank. A positive number in this column therefore suggest that the MHDI rank is better than that of HDI rank and a negative entry means the opposite.

In comparing the ranking orders by MHDI and HDI there seems to be little significant changes in the upper part of Appendix 1.

There are more notable changes in the upper-middle part of the table. Poland, Armenia, Antigua and Barbuda, Jamaica, Georgia, Azerbaijan, Romania, Albania, Kyrgyzstan and Seychelles gain from 7 to 10 ranks. Thailand, Bahrain, Mauritius, United Arab Emirates, Turkey and Brazil lose from 7 to 15 ranks.

In the lower-middle part of the table noticeable gainers are Uzbekistan, China, Dominican Republic, Jordan and Lebanon. Saudi Arabia, Syria, Tunisia, Iran, Libya, Botswana and Oman lose from 12 to 28 ranks.

The only noticeable changes in the lower part of the information in appendix 1 are Gabon and Solomon Islands each losing 8 ranks.

While the technical properties of the MHDI seem to be superior to those of the HDI, there does not seem to be a dramatic difference between their final outcomes.

To investigate the similarity between the rankings by MHDI and HDI we computed the Spearman rank correlation between them. This coefficient was 0.993 indicating significantly close ranking results by both indices.

Grouping of countries by the MHDI

The UNDP employs HDI for grouping countries into three categories of countries with high, medium and low levels of human development. It has been noted that the selected cut-off values of HDI have no justification, though an almost equal number of countries fall into each group (Kelley, 1991). In 1994 this grouping resulted in 53 countries being regarded as having high human development while 65 and 55 fell into medium and low groups, respectively.

As this grouping may have some bearing on the perception of people and perhaps decision makers of the level of human development in various countries[8], we decided to see how the MHDI may be used for this purpose.

The inspection of MHDI revealed sudden drops in the value of the index. The last column in Appendix 1 gives the decrease in consecutive values of MHDI. This figure seems to be high for certain countries which suggests a natural break at these levels. Bearing in mind that the mean of the MHDI is 0.577 and the mean of decrease in MHDI is 0.006 we took a fall in MHDI above three times its mean to be a significant drop. It is notable that this threshold of 0.018 is not repeated frequently. It resulted in 12 groups of countries at different levels of human development which are highlighted in Appendix 1.

The first break at the selected threshold belongs to Armenia. Countries above this country are a group of countries with a 'very high' level of human development. There are 45 countries in this group with an average MHDI of 0.902. Our next high group in Table 3 includes 7 countries from Armenia to Colombia. The average MHDI for this group is 0.802 still much above the average for all countries and slightly below the average of the previous group. We still regard the countries of this group to have a 'high' MHDI.

Fiji heads our third group which is the largest group consisting of 54 countries down to Guyana with a group average MHDI of 0.675 which is still well above the average for all countries. Members of this group may be regarded as enjoying a 'high-medium' level of human development, though the MHDI for the last few countries are below the average.

The remaining groups fall below the overall average value for MHDI. It is interesting to note that 9 out of 12 breaks at the selected threshold belongs to these countries indicating a rather high level of heterogeneity amongst them. These groups range from those with an average MHDI of 0.479 for El Salvador to Oman to the poorest, Benin to Sierra Leone, with the group average of 0.051.

171

Summary and conclusions

Despite regular improvements made in recent years, the HDI designed and published by the UNDP, has some serious shortcomings. They range from those related to the components of the index as well as those to do with the structure of the index itself.

The nature of some of these problems have been discussed and some suggestions have been made for improvement in both areas and took them into account to construct a modified version of human development index. The suggested MHDI takes into consideration the diminishing returns to the educational indicators. The structure of the index is improved in order to avoid the unintended scale effect which in turn is dependent on the subjectively selected extreme values for the components of the index.

The MHDI was applied to the data in HDR 1994 and the results were compared to those of the UNDP's HDI. It was demonstrated that while there is no dramatic differences in results, the technical properties of the new index are superior to those of the HDI. It was also demonstrated that the grouping of countries by the MHDI provides us with more distinct groups than those suggested by the UNDP's index.

Notes

1 In addition to the mentioned literature for one such attempt in the 1980s see McGranahan, et. al., 1985, though this was mainly a rework of the 1970 data.

2 The debate on the concept of development, however, has continued. For example see Sen, 1988 and 1990, Streeten, 1994 and Haq, 1995.

3 For Streeten, 1995 see the introductory chapter in Haq, 1995.

4 This treatment of Atkinson's formula in deriving the income component of HDI has been regarded by some researchers not to be in line with the original purpose of the formula (see Trablod-Nubler, 1991).

5 For a demonstration of such effects see Trabold-Nubler, 1991.

6 With the exception of the two constituent indicators of educational attainment which have arbitrarily selected unequal weights.

7 Hopkins (1991) goes further by stating that there is no *a priori* rationale for the simple addition of the components of HDI as they represent different concepts.

8 For an evidence of the ever increasing importance of the concept of human development in policy making, and inevitably its measure, see HDR 1995 (Box 6.4, p.121).

Appendix 1

The Modified Human Development Index

MHDI rank	Country	MHDI	HDI rank	HDIr - MHDIr	Decrease in MHDI
1	Switzerland	0.982	2	1	0.000
2	Sweden	0.979	4	2	0.003
3	Japan	0.978	3	0	0.002
4	Canada	0.976	1	-3	0.002
5	Norway	0.970	5	0	0.005
6	Netherlands	0.970	9	3	0.000
7	Australia	0.966	7	0	0.003
8	France	0.965	6	-2	0.002
9	Iceland	0.952	14	5	0.012
10	United Kingdom	0.951	10	0	0.002
11	USA	0.948	8	-3	0.003
12	Austria	0.948	12	0	0.000
13	Belgium	0.947	13	0	0.001
14	Germany	0.947	11	-3	0.001
15	Finland	0.941	16	1	0.006
16	Denmark	0.939	15	-1	0.002
17	Israel	0.938	19	2	0.001
18	New Zealand	0.937	18	0	0.001
19	Luxembourg	0.935	17	-2	0.002
20	Barbados	0.923	20	0	0.012
21	Ireland	0.917	21	0	0.006
22	Italy	0.909	22	0	0.008
23	Spain	0.903	23	0	0.007
24	Greece	0.889	25	1	0.014
25	Cyprus	0.887	26	1	0.002
26	Lithuania	0.881	28	2	0.006
27	Hong Kong	0.881	24	-3	0.001
28	Czechoslovakia	0.877	27	-1	0.004
29	Uruguay	0.867	33	4	0.009
30	Estonia	0.861	29	-1	0.006
31	Latvia	0.858	30	-1	0.003
32	Argentina	0.855	37	5	0.003
33	Costa Rica	0.851	39	6	0.003
34	Chile	0.851	38	4	0.001
35	Trinidad and Tobago	0.847	35	0	0.004

MHDI rank	Country	MHDI	HDI rank	HDIr - MHDIr	Decrease in MHDI
36	Korea Rep. of	0.847	32	-4	0.000
37	Hungary	0.847	31	-6	0.000
38	Bahamas	0.842	36	-2	0.005
39	Russian Federation	0.841	34	-5	0.001
40	Belarus	0.838	40	0	0.004
41	Malta	0.837	41	0	0.001
42	Poland	0.836	49	7	0.001
43	Bulgaria	0.832	48	5	0.004
44	Portugal	0.832	42	-2	0.000
45	Panama	0.828	47	2	0.004
46	**Armenia**	**0.808**	**53**	**7**	**0.020**
47	Antigua and Barbuda	0.807	55	8	0.001
48	Ukraine	0.804	45	-3	0.003
49	Singapore	0.803	43	-6	0.001
50	Brunei Darussalam	0.801	44	-6	0.002
51	Venezuela	0.798	46	-5	0.002
52	Colombia	0.793	50	-2	0.005
53	**Fiji**	**0.775**	**59**	**6**	**0.018**
54	Mexico	0.769	52	-2	0.006
55	Jamaica	0.769	65	10	0.000
56	Kuwait	0.766	51	-5	0.003
57	Kazakhstan	0.766	61	4	0.000
58	Georgia	0.764	66	8	0.002
59	Dominica	0.763	64	5	0.001
60	Malaysia	0.759	57	-3	0.004
61	Thailand	0.752	54	-7	0.007
62	Qatar	0.751	56	-6	0.001
63	Saint Vincent	0.743	69	6	0.009
64	Azerbaijan	0.742	71	7	0.000
65	Romania	0.742	72	7	0.000
66	Saint Kitts and Nevis	0.741	70	4	0.001
67	Bahrain	0.737	58	-9	0.003
68	Albania	0.734	76	8	0.004
69	Mauritius	0.724	60	-9	0.010
70	Maldova Rep. of	0.722	75	5	0.001
71	Saint Lucia	0.717	77	6	0.005
72	Grenada	0.713	78	6	0.004
73	United Arab Emirates	0.704	62	-11	0.010

MHDI rank	Country	MHDI	HDI rank	HDIr - MHDIr	Decrease in MHDI
74	Ecuador	0.703	74	0	0.000
75	Kyrgyzstan	0.689	82	7	0.014
76	Seychelles	0.687	83	7	0.002
77	Turkey	0.686	68	-9	0.001
78	Brazil	0.686	63	-15	0.000
79	Sri Lanka	0.685	90	11	0.001
80	Turkmenistan	0.684	80	0	0.001
81	Suriname	0.681	85	4	0.003
82	Paraguay	0.677	84	2	0.004
83	Belize	0.664	88	5	0.013
84	Uzbekistan	0.664	91	7	0.000
85	China	0.650	94	9	0.014
86	Saudi Arabia	0.649	67	-19	0.001
87	Cuba	0.649	89	2	0.000
88	Syrian Arab Rep.	0.643	73	-15	0.007
89	Dominican Rep	0.634	96	7	0.009
90	Jordan	0.628	98	8	0.006
91	Peru	0.625	95	4	0.003
92	Tajikestan	0.622	97	5	0.002
93	Tunisia	0.612	81	-12	0.011
94	Philippines	0.605	99	5	0.006
95	South Africa	0.605	93	-2	0.000
96	Lebanon	0.599	103	7	0.006
97	Korea Dem Rep	0.596	101	4	0.004
98	Iran, Islamic Rep	0.589	86	-12	0.007
99	Iraq	0.587	100	1	0.002
100	Libyan A J	0.585	79	-21	0.002
101	Mongolia	0.576	102	1	0.009
102	Samoa	0.572	104	2	0.004
103	Nicaragua	0.571	106	3	0.001
104	Botswana	0.566	87	-17	0.004
105	Indonesia	0.556	105	0	0.011
106	Guyana	0.553	107	1	0.003
107	**El Salvador**	**0.529**	**112**	**5**	**0.024**
108	Guatemala	0.523	108	0	0.006
109	Algeria	0.514	109	0	0.009
110	Honduras	0.507	115	5	0.007
111	Bolivia	0.497	113	2	0.010

MHDI rank	Country	MHDI	HDI rank	HDIr - MHDIr	Decrease in MHDI
112	Viet Nam	0.481	116	4	0.016
113	Morocco	0.478	111	-2	0.003
114	Maldives	0.474	118	4	0.005
115	Vanuatu	0.468	119	4	0.006
116	Egypt	0.462	110	-6	0.005
117	Swaziland	0.458	117	0	0.004
118	Cape Verde	0.446	122	4	0.012
119	Lesotho	0.437	120	1	0.009
120	Oman	0.433	92	-28	0.003
121	**Zimbabwe**	**0.411**	**121**	**0**	**0.023**
122	Gabon	0.408	114	-8	0.003
123	**Kenya**	**0.387**	**125**	**2**	**0.021**
124	Sao Tome and Principe	0.371	128	4	0.016
125	Cameroon	0.362	124	-1	0.009
126	Congo	0.350	123	-3	0.012
127	Myanmar	0.347	130	3	0.003
128	Papua New Guinea	0.336	129	1	0.011
129	Madagascar	0.327	131	2	0.008
130	India	0.325	135	5	0.002
131	Namibia	0.325	127	-4	0.001
132	Ghana	0.323	134	2	0.001
133	**Pakistan**	**0.294**	**132**	**-1**	**0.029**
134	Solomon Islands	0.291	126	-8	0.003
135	Haiti	0.286	137	2	0.005
136	Lao People's Dem. Rep.	0.285	133	-3	0.000
137	Cote d'Ivoire	0.278	136	-1	0.007
138	**Comoros**	**0.257**	**141**	**3**	**0.021**
139	Zaire	0.257	140	1	0.000
140	Nigeria	0.253	139	-1	0.004
141	**Liberia**	**0.230**	**144**	**3**	**0.023**
142	Zambia	0.228	138	-4	0.002
143	Togo	0.227	145	2	0.002
144	Tanzania	0.219	148	4	0.007
145	Yemen	0.209	142	-3	0.010
146	Bangladesh	0.200	146	0	0.010
147	Cambodia	0.191	147	0	0.009

MHDI rank	Country	MHDI	HDI rank	HDIr - MHDIr	Decrease in MHDI
148	Senegal	0.185	143	-5	0.005
149	**Burundi**	**0.163**	**152**	**3**	**0.022**
150	Nepal	0.162	149	-1	0.001
151	Equatorial Guinea	0.161	150	-1	0.001
152	Rwanda	0.156	153	1	0.005
153	**Angola**	**0.137**	**155**	**2**	**0.019**
154	Sudan	0.135	151	-3	0.001
155	Ethiopia	0.132	161	6	0.004
156	Malawi	0.125	157	1	0.006
157	Uganda	0.123	154	-3	0.002
158	Central African Rep	0.123	160	2	0.000
159	Bhutan	0.119	162	3	0.004
160	Mauritania	0.110	158	-2	0.009
161	Mozambique	0.110	159	-2	0.000
162	**Benin**	**0.083**	**156**	**-6**	**0.027**
163	Mali	0.068	167	4	0.015
164	Chad	0.067	168	4	0.001
165	Guinea-Bissau	0.066	164	-1	0.001
166	Niger	0.055	169	3	0.011
167	Somalia	0.054	165	-2	0.001
168	Gambia	0.052	166	-2	0.003
169	Djibouti	0.050	163	-6	0.002
170	Afghanistan	0.041	171	1	0.009
171	Burkina Faso	0.032	172	1	0.010
172	Guinea	0.024	173	1	0.008
173	Sierra Leone	0.019	170	-3	0.004
	Mean	0.577			0.006

References

Adelman, I. and Morris, C.T., (1967), *Society, Politics and Economic Development*, Baltimore, Johns Hopkins University Press.

Baster, N., (1985), 'Social Indicator Research: Some Issues and Debates', in Hilhorst and Klatter.

Chenery, H. et. al., (1976), *Redistribution With Growth*, Oxford, Oxford University Press.

Chenery, H. and Srinivasan, T.N., (1988), *Handbook of Development Economics Volume I*, Amsterdam, Elsevier Science Publishers.

Dasgupta, P. and Weale, M., (1992), 'On Measuring the Quality of Life', *World Development*, vol. 20, no. 1.

Desai, M., (1991), 'Human Development: Concept and Measurement', *European Economic Review*, 35.

Desai, M., (1993), 'Income and Alternative Measures of Well-Being', in Westendorff and Ghai, *Monitoring Social Progress in the 1990s*, UNRISD, Avebury, Aldershot.

Drewnowski, J. and Scott, W., (1966), 'The Level of Living Index', United Nations Research Institute for Social Development, Report No. 4, Geneva, United Nations.

Griffin, K. and Knight, J., (1990), *Human Development and the International Development Strategy for the 1990s*, London, Macmillan.

Haq, M.U., (1995), *Reflections on Human Development*, Oxford University Press.

Hicks, N. and Streeten, P., (1979), 'Indicators of Development: the Search for a Basic Needs Yardstick', *World Development*, vol. 7.

Hilhorst, J.G.M. and Klatter, M., (1985), *Social Development in the Third World*, London, Croom Helm.

Hopkins, M., (1991), 'Human Development Revisited: A New UNDP Report', *World Development*, Vol. 19, No. 10.

Kelley, A.C., (1991), 'The Human Development Index: Handle with Care', *Population and Development Review*, 17, No. 2.

McGillivray, M., (1991), 'The Human Development Index: Yet Another Redundant Composite Development Indicator?', *World Development*, Vol. 19, No. 10.

McGranahan, D.V. et. al., (1972), *Contents and Measurements of Socio-economic Development*, New York, Praeger.

McGranahan, D.V., Pizarro, P. and Richard, C., (1985), 'Measurement and Analysis of Socio-Economic Development', Geneva, United Nations Research Institute for Social Development.

Morris, M.D., (1979), *Measuring the Condition of the World's Poor: The Physical Quality of Life Index*, New York, Pergamon.

Murray, J.L., (1993), 'Development Data Constraints and the Human Development Index', in Westendorff and *Ghai Monitoring Social Progress in the 1990s*, UNRISD, Avebury, Aldershot.

Noorbakhsh, F., (1976), 'Development, Quantitative Analysis of Development and Planning for Development', PhD Thesis, University of Birmingham, United Kingdom.

Pyatt, G., (1992), 'There is nothing wrong with the HDI, but ...' Mimeo, University of Warwick.

Rao, V.V.B., (1991), 'Human Development Report 1990: Review and Assessment', *World Development*, vol.19, no. 10.

Rummel, R.J., (1970), 'Applied Factor Analysis', Evanston, Northwestern University Press.

Seers, D., (1972), 'What Are We Trying to Measure?', *The Journal of Development Studies*, vol.8, no. 3.

Sen, A., (1988), 'The Concept of Development', Chapter 1 in Chenery and Srinivasan, *Handbook of Development Economics Volume I*. Amsterdam, Elsevier Science Publishers.

Sen, A., (1990), 'Development as capability Expansion', Chapter 2 in Griffin and Knight, *Human Development and the International Development Strategy for the 1990s*, London, Macmillan.

Smith, P., (1993), 'Measuring Human Development', *Asian Economic Journal*, vol.7, no. 1.

Srinivasan, T.N., (1994), 'Human Development: A New Paradigm or Reinvention of the Wheel?', *American Economic Review, Papers and Proceedings*, vol. 84 no.2.

Streeten, P., Burki, J.S., Haq, M.U., Hicks, N. and Steward, F., (1981), *First Things first: Meeting basic human needs in developing countries*, New York, Oxford University Press.

Streeten, P., (1994), 'Human Development: Means and Ends', *American Economic Review, Papers and Proceedings*, vol. 84, no.2.

Trabold-Nubler, H., (1991), 'The Human Development Index - A New Development Indicator?', *Intereconomics*, September/October.

United Nations, (1954), 'Report on International Definition and Measurement of Standards and Levels of Living', New York, United Nations.

United Nations Economic and Social Council Commission for Social Development, (1969), 'Social Policy and Planning in National Development: Report of the Meeting of Experts on Social Policy and

Planning, held in Stockholm from 1 to 10 September, 1969', Geneva, United Nations

United Nations Development Programme (UNDP), (1990), *Human Development Report 1990*, Oxford University Press.

United Nations Development Programme (UNDP), (1991), *Human Development Report 1991*, Oxford University Press.

United Nations Development Programme (UNDP), (1992), *Human Development Report 1992*, Oxford University Press.

United Nations Development Programme (UNDP), (1993), *Human Development Report 1993*, Oxford University Press.

United Nations Development Programme (UNDP), (1994), *Human Development Report 1994*, Oxford University Press.

United Nations Research Institute for Social Development (UNRISD), (1972), *Contents and Measurement of Socio-economic Development*, New York, Praeger Publishers.

Westendorff, D.G. and Ghai, D., (1993), *Monitoring Social Progress in the 1990s*, UNRISD, Avebury, Aldershot.

World Bank, (1990), *World Development Report 1990: Poverty*, Oxford University Press.

12 Measuring and forecasting human resource needs in developing countries: SAM approach

Hossein Jalilian and Y. Yashar Sentürk

Introduction

Usefulness of resources, human or otherwise arise from the contribution that they could potentially make to the well being of a society. They are demanded because of their contribution to the production of goods and services which satisfy consumers' wants. Therefore, the forecast for any resource requirements, including human resources, could be based on the pattern and evolution of demand for goods and services which that particular resource(s) is a contributor.

In order to properly arrive at a level of demand for any particular input however, the mechanism within which that resource enters into productive activities need to be specified. The relationship between various inputs and output, and the way in which they are related, is usually captured by a 'production function'. Once the form of this production function is specified, any assumed changes in the demand for goods and services could also potentially provide a forecast for the future requirement of resources. This is the principle which is used in this chapter to determine any resource need within a particular setting.

Degree of relative accuracy of forecasting varies with the extent of sophistication of 'models' imposed on the system. In the case of the resource needs for example, an econometrics model could be set up which is composed of system of equations, each of which behaviorally determining output, factor input demand, factor input supply and the like, thus taking full account of market environment and prices. This procedure however, may be too demanding in terms of resources and data. Alternatively, it could be argued that under circumstances that most developing countries operate, there may be no additional gains from this kind of modelling approach. Due to these limitations, as well as other specific characteristics of developing countries in general, quantitative research in these areas, particularly at macro level, have been limited to the use of few modelling tools, including Input-Output (IO), Social Accounting Matrices (SAM), and to a lesser degree Computable General Equilibrium (CGE).

Limitations of IO modelling are well known. Though some of these limitations extend to the SAM, the structure of the latter are more appropriate given the context of many developing countries. Data scarcity still limits application of CGE to many developing countries. The approach which has been adopted here is that of SAM. The rest of the paper organised as following: In section II we provide a brief description of production functions in general and their relation to SAM. Then, in section III we look at the composition and structure of SAMs. In the section IV the SAM's usefulness for policy analysis as well as a forecasting tool are investigated. Finally section V provides a summary and concludes our discussion.

Production function approach

Any productive activity is likely to involve utilisation of different categories of services of human inputs, such as managerial, technical, as well as broad categories of different levels of skilled, semi-skilled and unskilled labour. Another important factor input is that of capital, which like labour is composed of different forms of fixed and variable capital of different degree of vintage and sophistication. These, combined with variety of other primary factor inputs, such ass different quality and quantity of raw materials, energy, as well as some intermediate products, results in different forms of products and services produced within an economy. The way in which various combination of inputs are combined in order to produce a given level of product or service could be approximated by a production function. The production function in (1) is an implicit form of one such relationships.

$$Q_t = f(R_{ijt}) \qquad i=1.....n, \; j=1.....m, \; t=1.....T \qquad (1)$$

In the above formulation 'Q' stands for output, and 'R' for resources. Subscript 'i' specifies different broad category of resources used in productive process, such as labour, capital, raw material and energy; 'j' specifies the sub category of resource 'i', such as different forms of labour, capital, raw material etc.; and 't' denotes different time periods. The production function approach could, under appropriate assumptions, be applied to micro- and macro level studies, in order to specify production function for a particular sector, industry, region or the macro-economy level for each of the respective category of economic activities.

The implicit functional form such as specified above, though appropriate for theoretical discussions, is not much of a help for empirical studies and policy analysis. For the latter purposes, the functional form need to be explicitly specified. In which case the theory which underlines the particular specification could be tested against available data. In many cases, however, data availability is such that the applied investigation of the broad spectrum of theoretical specification and modelling may not be feasible. This is particularly the case with many of the developing countries; data available in most is relatively limited both in terms of quality and quantity. In such a situation modelling specification to a large extent is governed by data availability and reliability. One such approach which maximises data utilisation as well as acting as a consistency framework for data, is SAM, which will be dealt with below.

SAM: components and structure

Analysis of interactions among sectors and institutions in the economy is a key to understanding, assessing, appraising and formulating the success or otherwise of the policies pursued by the government, given its objectives set forth in the development plans. Such multi-sectoral analysis, through their various applications are also able to 'assess the economywide effects, for instance, of an increase in demand for one sector, or in external transfers to an institution, are useful means for projection and forecasting purposes (Sadoulet, E., and de Janvry, A., 1995; p. 273).

As the name suggests the sector based modelling exercises attempt to formalise the workings of and the interrelationships between one or more sectors of an economy and the policy changes that have come about in the country (or region), with a view to focusing on the impact of the latter on the socio-economic fabrics of the society, that is the households, via their effects on the sectors considered.

IO and SAM are important examples of multi-sectoral models. In the development literature, the usefulness of IO analysis and SAM have been frequently cited (Pyatt and round, 1985; Thorbecke, 1985; Thirlwall, 1990; Sadoulet and de Janvry, 1995), for purposes of planning, projection and forecasting the future factor requirements for an economy.

In a nutshell, SAM is a unified way to present a set of accounts for an economy that describes the circular flow (Pyatt and Round, 1985; Thorbecke, 1985; Robinson, 1986; Adelman and Robinson, 1988). In its basic form it is a square matrix in which, as in IO, the rows depict the receipts and the columns depict the expenditures for as many groups which needs to be specified. Within this framework human resources such as labour of various skills, such as white or blue-collar workers, professionals, agricultural labour, semi-skilled labour all enter into the factors accounts, and in some cases into the socio-economic group classifications.

As a methodological instrument, Thorbecke (1985) notes that 'the SAM is an essential tool in diagnosing the initial situation and in organising the data in a systematic way with respect to accounts, classification and the interrelationships of the variables appearing in these accounts'. At the same time, by itself SAM is a data framework which is a snapshot in time, yielding base-year information in a consistent way among a whole set of variables.

There is an interesting relation between the SAM and formal models. Although not a fully formalised model, SAM analysis appears to be a macroeconomic stepping process in the direction of creation of formal modelling. In another word, it can be said that 'modelling is a major area of application of SAMs' (Pyatt and Round, 1985).

A typical SAM contains the following set of accounts:

- *Production sectors/activities* (e.g. staple-crops, export-crops, perennial-crops, livestock, fibers, various non-agricultural sectors as manufacturing, services and financial, utilities);
- *Factors of Production* (labour and capital of different types) that receive, as income, the value added by the production sectors;
- *Institutions*, such as households, firms;
- *Capital accounts*, to receive savings and make investment;
- *Government*; and the
- *Rest of the world* accounts.

The flow of products between the productive sectors are represented by an input-output table. In this respect, a SAM can also be viewed as an expanded input-output matrix to which has been added the flows of the producing activities to the primary factors (the value added); the flows from these factors to institutions such as households (in the form of income for factor-services), and governments (in the form of taxes), and eventually completing the circular flow of funds in the economy by tracing the demand for goods from the producing sector generated by households, governments, and foreign residents.

The SAM approach serves to emphasise the fact that the distribution of employment opportunities and living standards in a society is inextricably interwoven with the structure of production and the distribution of resources. Hence, the question of 'who gets what, and how much, as a result of the economic process of income generation' is set in the context of a conventional national accounts and input-output analysis, with data displayed in the single entry matrix format which is essential to SAM and distinguishes it from the more traditional forms of double-entry bookkeeping.

The advantage of the SAM is that it captures the flows across markets where movement of commodities or factor services is matched by a corresponding payment-flow in the reverse direction. Of particular importance in the present context is the fact that in addition, the financial flows which have no counterparts are also captured by the SAM (Robinson, 1986). These include, for example, the payment of transfers from government to household sector. Remittances from foreign to domestic residents, or internal remittances from one group of households to another can also be represented explicitly within this framework.

Further benefits of SAM over alternative representations of data stem from the fact that it is a relatively well-disaggregated system. That is, each transaction has an identifiable account-origin and account-destination, which facilitates for better understanding of the generation, transmission, distribution, and redistribution of income and subsequent expenditure mechanisms within an economy. Moreover, the aggregate transactions between these accounts are relatively self-explanatory from the table. Thus for example, table 12.1. gives a simplified SAM framework representation where the factor accounts receive value added from domestic production activities (cell 1,3) and from abroad (workers' remittances) (cell 1,4b), and pay these factor income receipts to the institutions according to their ownership of factors of production. In this respect, households receive labour income in return for the labour services provided, whereas the companies (public or private) receive operating surpluses before any deduction for depreciation, taxes, etc ... and some factor incomes paid abroad.

In a simplified Social Accounting Matrix, the main structure of accounts, together with the border totals, are as follows.

Factors of production consist primarily of the capital and labour used in the process of production. But the production process draws these accounts from where it can, without being concerned with the entities to which their owners belong. Within this context, these entities constitute the institutions accounts to which households, firms, and government accounts belong.

185

Being an extended version of IO table, SAM is in a way inextricably linked to the workings of the IO analysis, although it is a more substantial and useful methodology for planning purposes. Encompassing the IO inter-industry matrix as one of its components, SAM makes it possible to calculate how much of commodities X_1, ... n will be required at some future date, given a certain growth rate of national income or final demand. Such information helps human resource planners and managers to achieve consistency in planning, anticipate the types of factors that may be needed in future and avoid future bottlenecks in the productive process.

As one of the important cornerstones in the circular flow of effects of a given policy change on factor requirements, the inter-industry matrix shown below (table 12.2.) presents not only the interrelationships between the various sectors of the economy, but also the allocation of resources amongst sectors, and factors of production. In many developing countries, if development level is to change to a higher trajectory, then macro-economic policy reforms must ensure a more efficient domestic resource mobilisation and knowledge of future human resource and other factor requirements. Within this perspective SAM brings into the attention of the developers, planners and policy-makers, the state of the inter-exchange of resources within the economy at a snapshot in time. Further, it also helps for forecasting the possible labour/raw materials requirements (be it sectoral, or for the whole economy). This aspect of the SAM will be dealt with later.

In Table 12.2., X_{ij} denotes sales by industry i to industry j or inputs into industry j from industry i, where $I=1$, ... n, and $j=1$, ... n. The disposal of outputs to final users is represented in the same way. Also in the table above I refers to Investment, E stands for exports, TD for total demand and TS for total supply.

As mentioned earlier, SAM is in effect a single-entry accounting system whereby each macroeconomic account is represented by a column for outgoings and a row for incomings. An entry, for example in i,j^{th} cell represents the transaction which is a receipt by the ith account from account j (or expenditures by account j that are paid out to account I). Below the main application areas of SAM in forecasting the effects of a given policy change and its consequent final demand/output change on the factors of production are investigated.

Table 12.1
A simplified SAM structure

RECEIPTS	EXPENDITURES			Other Accounts		TOTAL
	1 Factors	2 Institutions*	3 Production Activities	4 Combined Capital	Rest of the World	
1 Factors			Factoral Income Distribution ($T_{1,3}$)			Income of Factors
2 Institutions*	Income Distr. To Households & other institutions ($T_{2,1}$)	Transfers, Taxes, and Subsidies ($T_{2,2}$)			Receipts of the Institutions from the Rest of the World	Income of Institutions
3 Production Activities		Institutional Demand for Goods & Services ($T_{3,2}$)	Intermediary Demand ($T_{3,3}$)	Gross Capital Formation	Exports	Gross Demand
4 Combined Aggregate Capital		Domestic Savings			Balance of Payments Current Account Deficit	Total Savings
Rest of the World		Imports of Competitive Goods	Imports of Complimentary Goods			Total Foreign Exchange Outflow
TOTAL	Outlay (Income) of Factors	Expenditures of Institutions	Gross Output	Total Aggregate Investment	Total Foreign Exchange Inflow	

Source: Thorbecke, E., (1985).

187

Table 12.2
A typical input-output (IO) table

Sales by / Purchases by	Intermediate Users			Final Demand				
	INDUSTRIES			Consumption		I	E	TD
	1	j	n	Private (C)	Government (G)			
1	X_{11}	X_{1j}	X_{1n}	X_{1C}	X_{1G}	X_{1I}	X_{1E}	X_1
I	X_{i1}	X_{ij}	X_{in}	X_{iC}	X_{iG}	X_{iI}	X_{iE}	X_i
n	X_{n1}	X_{nj}	X_{nn}	X_{nC}	X_{nG}	X_{nI}	X_{nE}	X_n
Wages (W)	W_1	W_j	W_n	W_C	W_G			W
Rent (R)	R_1	R_j	R_n	R_C	R_G			R
Interest (D)	D_1	D_j	D_n	D_C	D_G			D
Profits (P)	P_1	P_j	P_n	P_C	P_G			P
Imports (M)	M_1	M_j	M_n	M_C	M_G	M_I	M_E	M
TS	X_1	X_j	X_n	C	G	I	E	

Source: Thirlwall, A.P., (1990).

Policy analysis and forecasting under SAM

The simplest and the most direct way to create a model of the economic processes based on SAM is through the 'Multiplier Analysis'. This allows us to predict how changes in some elements of the matrix will be reflected in changes of other flows. The changes in the final demand are translated to changes in the incomes of households by solving for the multipliers based on the static coefficients derived from a SAM. The coefficients are computed by dividing each element in the column by the column sum under the assumption that 'they remain fixed over time'. For this reason, it is important to define those accounts in a manner which makes feasible the fact that 'the expenditure coefficients are constant over the length of period contemplated'. However, as the SAM is a square matrix, and the coefficients in every column must sum up to unity, there is 'no the inverse' to the matrix. The problem is only resolved by specifying that one or more of the accounts in the SAM is exogenous. Obvious ones are: the government account, foreign (rest of the world) account, and capital account.

The application of the multiplier analysis with a complete SAM takes into account all the interactions within each step of the process of linkages among incomes, expenditures, and production. the linkages could also include the effects on other industries of expansion within a particular industry. This, as opposed to a single multiplier provides an entire set of multipliers which potentially shows the effect of expansion in one cell of the original SAM on any other cell.

Several different applications of this latter type of multiplier analysis have been made which are described in the Pyatt and Round (1985). One such study is the Botswana SAM, where the SAM relationships can trace the complex interactions inherent in the circular process. If initial changes in prices or wages are involved, the analysis can show, at least in orders of magnitude, how the initial changes affect the prices in different industrial sectors and consumption patterns of different household groups. Such analysis, however, are based at first on the assumption that patterns of production and consumption are not affected by price changes. Adaptation to take into account the assumed responses can, however, be introduced which is essential in the modelling of an economy.

In order to determine how a given policy change, in the labour market, affects the final demand/output, and the way this feeds on in the circular process of production, it is essential to understand the workings of the multiplier analysis within the SAM structure. For example, in the case of price liberalisation, by extending the IO to include flow-of-funds from functions to institutions and between institutions, SAM also helps to analyse the institutional/functional income distribution. A SAM is then constructed on a disaggregated basis in order to have the maximum benefit from data and distribution parameters. This implies that in the case of factors, labour and capital accounts (see Table 12.1) are further disaggregated into subcategories. In the case of human resource indexing we will take labour accounts disaggregated into skilled, semi-skilled and unskilled labour. Each of these could be further disaggregated into its constituent parts. In the case of skilled labour for example, this could be further disaggregated into its various components including managerial, technical and administrative. In the same way, the capital account could be subdivided into fixed and variables of different forms and vintages. With such disaggregations in the factor accounts, planning by way of forecasting the future needs based on changes in the policy/ final demand/ output parameters in the system can be investigated with a greater degree of reliability.

Mathematical structure of SAM

First stage in this investigation involves setting up the framework of main transactions table, followed by the derivation of the technical coefficients which is obtained by dividing each transaction in the table by its column sum,

$$a_{ij} = X_{ij} / X_j \qquad (2)$$

Each row total in that case can be written as:

$$X_i = \sum_i a_{ij} X_j + Y_i \qquad (3)$$

Or in matrix notation form we have:

$$X = AX + Y \qquad (4)$$

which provides the general solution for the final vector of output X in terms of technical coefficient matrix A and the final demand vector Y, as follows:

$$X = (I-A)^{-1} Y \qquad (5)$$

where I represents the identity matrix and $(I-A)^{-1}$ is the so called 'Leontief inverse'. Equation (5) states that given technical coefficient matrix A, it is the level of final demand for goods and services that determines final output X_i, at the aggregate level; the aggregation being at the level of industry, region or the country.

Instead of determining the level, rate of change in final output, ΔX, can also be written as:

$$\Delta X = (I-A)^{-1} \Delta Y \qquad (6)$$

that is to say, any change in final demand generates corresponding level of changes in the final output of endogenous accounts; or alternatively we have:

$$\Delta X / \Delta Y = (I-A)^{-1} \qquad (7)$$

(7) is the familiar multiplier.

The RHS of (7) could be approximated as

$$(I-A)^{-1} = I + \sum_{i=1}^{n} A^i \qquad (8)$$

Alternatively, the Leontief inverse represents sum of the successive rounds of output requirements, in order to satisfy the initial shock to the system represented by the change in final demand for goods and services. This is composed of the initial change in demand represented by I, the second round of changes in order to satisfy the initial change in demand, represented by A; the third round, in order to satisfy the change in output required at the second round of change generated in the second round, represented by A^2, and so on. For a medium size IO table, the first five or six round of changes provides a good approximation to the Leontief inverse.

Thus, the column sum of the Leontief inverse provides the total sectoral multiplier represented by that column; and the total row sum, the total sectoral output change for simultaneous unit change in final demand for all sectors. Of diagonal elements of the Leontief inverse provides the indirect multipliers and the diagonal elements those of direct ones.

In the same way the change in the exogenous accounts of the SAM, L, can be determined given as follows:

$$\Delta L = B(I-A)^{-1} \Delta Y \qquad (9)$$

where B is a (k x n) matrix of technical coefficient of exogenous account and their interaction with endogenous ones.

Forecasting the skilled-labour requirements

By employing SAM, forecasting the human resource requirements becomes a straightforward task. Any perceived policy change and their likely impact on final demand for goods and services is imposed on the system to drive the final output requirements to satisfy the change in the final demand. In order to do so, derived demand for factors of production would have to change. As in the production activities, assuming that the proportionality between the output and inputs remains the same, this will give us approximate change in demand for any particular input. By running several scenarios and running sensitivity analysis, one would arrive at a range of values for a particular resource.

In the case of human resources of type 'I' for example, to satisfy the new set of final output required by (6), each ΔX_j generates $r_{ij}\Delta X_{ij}$ of demand for 'i' resource for each 'j' activity. therefore, the total change in the demand for resource R_i can be calculated as follows:

$$\Delta R_i = \sum_{j=1}^{n} r_{ij} \Delta X_{ij} \qquad (10)$$

191

where r_{ij} represents factor resource requirements of type 'i' in order to produce an extra unit of product type 'j'. Depending on the level of disaggregation of resource accounts in the SAM, such as classification in terms of skill, task, hierarchy, specific nature of change in demand for each resource required could be calculated. In general, the required change in vector of factor resources resulting from a change in final demand can be derived from the following relationship:

$$\Delta R = r (I-A)^{-1} \Delta F \qquad (11)$$

where R specifies vector of factor resource, and r the matrix of technical coefficients which signify the interaction of resources with endogenous accounts in the SAM.

Summary and conclusion

Although a major use of multiplier analyses in the SAM framework has been for the analysis of the income distribution policy (Thorbecke, 1985; Hayden and Round, 1982; and Khan and Thorbecke, 1988), as argued here it can also be a major analytical tool in development planning in the context of determining the human resource requirements.

One issue that needs to be more fully considered is the qualitative nature of the variables involved, especially within the context of human resources. The exact nature of the interaction between quality of a resource and the quantitative outcome of its interaction is difficult, if not impossible, to formulate.

It is useful to sum up some of the limitations of SAM as a policy analysis tool. Like IO, SAM is demand driven. The underlined assumption is that there are spare capacities within the system that could easily be utilised as demand increases. This, especially within developing countries' context, is rather a strong assumption. SAM is also a 'fixed coefficient model', where price variations do not play any role in resource allocation. Although they may not be too restrictive in terms of providing a snapshot of interaction between variables, this may not extend to comparisons over time and forecasting. For the latter, a more dynamic analytical framework is required. In general, the framework is incapable of incorporating price variation as a policy tool. Although the more sophisticated dynamic modelling and the extension of SAM to CGE modelling relaxes some of these shortcomings, they generate their own problems.

As in many issues relating to developing countries, however, one may not be much short of analytical frameworks and tools, but rather too limited in terms of quality and quantity of data available to test these. Given the flexibility of SAM and IO in terms of structure and data use relative to others, they could be set up to suit the data available. Information provided by using analytical tools such as SAM in that case will still be very useful for policy analysis such as human resource planning, but they should be taken as an indicative rather than precise measure of parameters of interest.

References

Adelman, I., and Robinson, S., (1988), 'Macroeconomic Adjustment and Income Distribution: Alternative Models Applied to Two Economies', *Journal of Development Economics*, vol. 29.

Amjad, R., Colclough, D., Garcia, N., Hopkins, N., Infante, R., and Rodgers, G., (1990), *Quantitative Techniques in Employment Planning*, ILO, Geneva.

Cohen, S. I., (1987), 'Input-Output Versus Social Accounting in the Macro-analysis of Development Policy', *Industry and Development*, Part 22.

Ferroni, M., and Grootaert, C., (1993), 'Policy Reform: concepts, Data, Analysis', in Demery, L., et. al. (eds), *Understanding the Social Effects of Policy Reform*, A World Bank Study, Washington, D.C.

Greenfield, C. G., (1985), 'A SAM for Botswana, 1974-1975', in Pyatt, G., and Round, J. I., *Social Accounting Matrices: A Basis for Planning*, A World Bank Symposium, World Bank, Washington, D.C.

Hayden, C., and Round, J., (1982), 'Developments in Social Accounting Methods as Applied to the Analysis of Income Distribution and Employment Issues', *World Development*, vol 10.

Hirschman, A. O., (1958), *The Strategy of Economic Development*, Yale University Press, New Haven.

Khan, H., and Thorbecke, E., (eds) (1989), 'Macroeconomic Effects of Technology Choice: Multiplier and Structural Path Analysis within a SAM Framework', *Journal of Policy Modeling*, vol. 11.

King, B.B., (1985), 'What is SAM?', in Pyatt, G., and Round, J., *Social Accounting Matrices: A Basis for Planning*, A World Bank Symposium, World Bank, Washington, D.C.

Muqtada, M., and Hildeman, A. (eds) (1993), *Labour Markets and Human Resource Planning in Asia: Perspectives and Evidence*, ILO, Geneva.

Muqtada, M., (1993), 'Manpower Planning, Labour Markets Analysis and Human Resource Development', Planning: An Introductory Note', in

Muqtada, M., and Hildeman, A. *Labour Markets and Human Resource Planning in Asia: Perspectives and Evidence*, ILO, Geneva.

Muqtada, M., and Hildeman, A., (1993), 'Labour Markets and Human Resource Planning: An Introductory Note', in Muqtada, M., and Hildeman, A. *Labour Markets and Human Resource Planning in Asia: Perspectives and Evidence*, ILO, Geneva.

Palm, F. C., and Smit, H.D., (1991), *Economic Modelling and Policy Analysis*, Avebury, Aldershot.

Papola, T.S., (1993), 'Labour Market Monitoring for Employment Planning: A Framework Illustrated with the Indian Experience', in Muqtada, M., and Hildeman, A. *Labour Markets and Human Resource Planning in Asia: Perspectives and Evidence*, ILO, Geneva.

Pyatt, G., and Round, J. I., (eds), (1985), *Social Accounting Matrices: A Basis for Planning*, A World Bank Symposium, World Bank, Washington, D.C.

Quizon, J., and Binswanger, H., (1986), 'Modelling the Impact of Agricultural Growth and Government Policy on Income Distribution in India', *World Bank Economic Review*, vol.1.

Roe, A., (1985), 'Flow of Funds as a Tool of Analysis in Developing Countries', in Pyatt, G., and Round, J., *Social Accounting Matrices: A Basis for Planning*, A World Bank Symposium, World Bank, Washington, D.C.

Round, J., (1984), 'Income Distribution Within a Social Accounting Matrix: A Review of Some Experience in Malaysia and Other LDCs', in Nissen, H. P. (ed.), *Towards Income Distribution Policies*, University of Paderborn, Dept. of Economics, EADI - Book Series, No.3, Tilburg.

Sadoulet, E., and de Janvry, A., (1995), *Quantitative Development Policy Analysis*, The Johns Hopkins University Press, London.

Scobie, G. M., (1989), *Macroeconomic Adjustment and the Poor: Toward a Research Policy*, Cornell Food and Nutrition Programme, monog.1.

Thorbecke, E., (1985), The Social Accounting Matrix and Consistency-type. Planning Models', in Pyatt, G., and Round, J. I., *Social Accounting Matrices: A Basis for Planning*, A World Bank Symposium, World Bank, Washington, D.C.

Thirlwall, A.P., (1990), *Growth and Development: with special reference to developing economies*, (4th ed.), Macmillan, London.

For Product Safety Concerns and Information please contact our EU
representative GPSR@taylorandfrancis.com Taylor & Francis Verlag GmbH,
Kaufingerstraße 24, 80331 München, Germany

Printed and bound by CPI Group (UK) Ltd, Croydon, CR0 4YY
08/05/2025
01864370-0004